THE

POSTHUMOUS WORKS

OF

ANNE RADCLIFFE,

AUTHORESS OF THE MYSTERIES OF UDOLPHO, &c.

COMPRISING

GASTON DE BLONDEVILLE, A ROMANCE;

St. Alban's Abbey, a Metrical Tale,

WITH VARIOUS POETICAL PIECES.

———

TO WHICH IS PREFIXED

A MEMOIR OF THE AUTHORESS,
WITH EXTRACTS FROM HER PRIVATE JOURNALS.

———

IN FOUR VOLUMES.

VOL. IV.

———

LONDON:

PUBLISHED FOR HENRY COLBURN,
BY R. BENTLEY, NEW BURLINGTON STREET.
—
1833.

CONTENTS

OF THE FOURTH VOLUME.

Page.

ST. ALBAN'S ABBEY, CONTINUED:
Canto X.   Among the Dead   .   .   . 1
Notes to St. Alban's Abbey   .   .   . 45

MISCELLANEOUS POEMS.

Salisbury Plains—Stonehenge   109
Shakspeare's Cliff   162
The Fishers—Steephill   170
In the New Forest   178
On a First View of the Group called "The Seven Moun-
    tains"   181
A Second View of the Seven Mountains   .   . 183
On ascending a Hill crowned with a Convent, near Bonn . 185
The Snow-Fiend   192
An Ancient Beech-tree in the Park at Knole—The Wood-
    land Nymph   .   :   .   .   . 196
Sea-Views—Midnight   200
To the Swallow   204
Forest Lawns   206
On the Rondeau "Just like Love is yonder Rose"   . 209
December's Eve, Abroad   211
December's Eve, at Home   213

	Page.
A Sea-View	215
On Hayley's " Life of Cowper" . . .	220
Written in the Isle of Wight . . .	221
Sonnet to the Lark	231
On Lines by Lady Elizabeth Lee, in a Bower at St. Leo-	
nard's Hill	232
To the River Dove	236
The Sea-mew	240
To the Winds	249
Moonlight: A Scene. . . .	251
Smiles	253
The Reed of Poesy . . .	256
EDWY: a Poem, in Three Parts.	
Part I. The Hazel Tree—A Summer Song of Fairie ..	259
II. The Fairie Court—A Summer's Night in Wind-	
sor Park	273
III. The Magic Mirrors—A Summer's Night in Wind-	
sor Forest . . .	310
Scene on the Northern Shore of Sicily . .	329

CANTO X.

AMONG THE DEAD.

I.

WITH even step and shaded eye
Florence the tombs now passes by.
While near the choir Fitzharding drew,
Pausing, he points out to her view
Where the three noble warriors lie,
With high and solemn obsequy
Of torches fixed and priestly ward,
And incense-cloud and herald-guard.

II.

By the first bier he took his stand,
And looked on great Northumberland,
Kinsman of Hotspur—him, who died
Fighting against the new-grown pride
Of Bolingbroke, whose wiles and might
Usurped the second Richard's right;

Kinsman of him, who blazed the deed
Of Richard's death in Pomfret tower,
Defying the usurper's power.
And now had Hotspur's kinsman died,
Fighting on that usurper's side ;
Yet for a meek and blameless king,
To whom his unsought honours bring,
The curse of his progenitor,
Disputed right and civil war.

III.

Dashing aside a soldier's tear,
Fitzharding reached the centre bier ;
Portcullis yet was watchful here.
He looked on his commander's face,
And thought within how short a space
He had himself obeyed his voice,
   Soon as the battle-hour began,
Flattered and honoured, by his choice,
   With post of danger in the van.
Then every limb with life was warm ;
Now heavy death pressed all his form,
Its sullen gloom hung on his brow,
And tinged the half-closed lid below,

Dwelt in the hollow of his cheek,
And seemed, with breathless sign, to speak
Of more than human tongue may dare—
·Of the last pang, that lingered there.

IV.

His dinted casque, that stood beside,
Told whence had rushed the fatal tide;
Its high plume, that had waved so gay
Beneath St. Alban's tower this day,
Mantling like snowy swan, and danced
To every step his charger pranced;
As jocund at the trumpet's air,
And proud the pomps of war to share,—
Now broken, stained, and stiff with gore
Fell, as in horrors, bristled o'er.
The golden lions in his shield
    Glared on his pulseless breast;
And every sign, that rank revealed
    And royal race professed,
    Seemed but to mock his rest.
His honours now—the pausing eye,
The people's tear, the warrior's sigh;

For these alone his virtues tell :—
Grandson of John o' Gaunt, farewell!

v.

Fitzharding, with swift step, passed on
To the third bier, which stood alone ;
And here—oh here ! the pausing eye—
The sudden tear—the bursting sigh,
　At once De Clifford own.
Oh loyal heart ! oh brave old man !
And hast thou closed thy mortal span,
With youthful fire, exhaustless zeal
For thy good king and country's weal !
And, scorning age and shadowy days,
Hast, with the eagle's dauntless gaze,
Still soared in Glory's keenest blaze,
And won a circlet of her rays !—
Awhile Fitzharding bent his head,
In mindful stillness, o'er the dead—
Then turned upon his dreadful way,
To seek if thus his father lay :
While the deep thunder's mystic groan
Muttered, it seemed, prophetic moan !

VI.

With eager eye he sought around,
Through the black shades of this drear ground,
And, while the lightning quivering throws
It's pale glance o'er each warrior's brows,
Catches each shape and look of death
Extended on the graves beneath.
How sudden rose each livid face
From forth the shadows of the place,
    And, sudden sunk, was seen no more—
The vision with the blue glimpse o'er !
And often to his anxious view
Thus rose some form in death he knew:
One who had close beside him fought,
While Richard's fiercest self he sought ;
Some who had near his father been,
When in the throng he last was seen,
And when from battle he in vain
Had sought to join his band again.

VII.

On a low stone, lit up by ray
Of single torch, a body lay

In ringed mail ; with umbered gleam
Full on the face red flashes stream.
Fitzharding paused awhile, and groaned,
Again his eye a comrade owned ;
For whom high danger he had braved ;
Whose life, that day, he once had saved.
His iron van-brace now could show
The very dint of sabre blow,
Aimed at the life he then preserved,
Alas ! for speedy fate reserved.

VIII.

Where spread each graven brass, beyond,
    Above, below, was death ;
Above, scarce cold, a warrior's hand,
    A monk's lay hid beneath,
That had for ages mouldered there,
Since he had left his cell of care.
Such brass-sealed grave showed sculpture rude
Of monk, in kneeling attitude.
There lay the brave Sir Robert Vere,
Whose words yet smote Fitzharding's ear,
" Warwick breaks up the Barrier !"

With winged speed he urged his way,
Then plunged in thickest of the fray.

IX.

And here, among the loyal slain,
   Behold! Sir Richard Fortescue;
There lay Sir William Chamberlain;
   There, Sir Ralph Ferrers, brave and true;
With many a veteran knight and squire,
Whose breast had flamed with patriot fire;
And humbler men, whose courage high
Had taught them for their prince to die.
Who now shall wait at the King's gate,
      For, here lies faithful Chanselar?*
Who urge the steed to utmost speed,
      For Henry Hawlin† sleepeth here?
Of all the wide lands he has traced
      Six feet for him remain;
Of all the minutes of his haste
      Not one to tell his pain!

* Richard Chanselar, porter to Henry VI.
† Henry Hawlin, a messenger of " our lady, Dame Mar_
garett."

To other tongue he leaves to say
Tiding of Alban's bloody fray;
To bear unto Queen Margaret's ears
The crowded tale of woes and fears—
Pressed into hours the fate of years!
His course, his toilful bustle done,
Now lies he here—HIS INN IS WON.

x.

And who shall to the dais bring,
With marshalled state before the King,
   And train of HOUSEHOLD SQUIRES,
   And blaze of YEUL-CLOUGH FIRES,
The boar's head, at that merry tide,
When royal halls are opened wide?
Not he so mute on yonder grave;
   The King's chief Sewer he;—
Never again his chaunted stave
   Shall join the minstrelsy!
Never again his jocund eye
Shall glance where banners wave on high,
And where plumed knight and ladies bright
Are ranged around, in purple dight—

Knights, who no more in gallant state
  Shall answer to the minstrel's call;
Ladies, whom war and cruel fate
  Have banished from the lighted hall.

XI.

But who is he, within the shade
Of Wulphstan's ancient altar laid?
No funeral torch, with lurid glare,
Burns o'er the iron warrior there;
Nor watch-monk sits in piteous care.
But twilight rays from distant tomb
Just shape his outline through the gloom.—
  Whence is the tremour Florence feels?
Why does Fitzharding grasp her arm,
Silent and shaking with alarm?—
  He fears dread truth that bier conceals.
In vain he bends upon the face,
Yet seems his father's form to trace.
He signed the monk, attendant still,
  To hasten where yon glimmers lead,
  For the lone torch, his fate to read.
Yet, while the monk obeyed his will,

B 5

He feared lest sudden lightning-glance
Might show his father's countenance
Sunk ghastly in the helm and drear.
He turned him from such awful chance,
And dimly saw, beside the bier,
A form in silence resting near,
In other cares so wrapped was he,
He guessed not now of treachery.

XII.

" Oh ! will these moments never fleet ?
  Yet for this slow monk must I wait ?"
He made some hasty steps to meet
  His lingering messenger of fate ;
And seized the torch, with desperate hand,
And took again his fearful stand.
The flame glanced o'er the golden crest ;
And there the leopard stood confessed !
The face !—he turned him from the light,
Veiling his eyes from the dread sight,
To meet that altered look afraid.
Sudden, strong hands the torch invade,
And hold it forth upon the corpse.

He turned to see what stranger's force
Had seized it.   There, with bending head,
A form looked on the warrior dead ;
And, as he viewed the corpse below,
The torch flashed full upon his brow,
And showed his quivering lip, his eye,
Fixed as by some dire phantasie.
Then, all his father's look was known,
Reflecting terrors like his own
While that dead form he gazed upon,
And feared to find his slaughtered son !
The living voice beside him spoke !
The long-fixed spell at once was broke !

XIII.

But who may tell the feelings high
Rising from fear to ecstasy,
While sire and son each other pressed,
And each in other's grasp was blessed.
Their joy was as the Morning's smile,
  With light of heaven upon its brow,
The sable wreaths of Night, the while,
  Frowning upon the world below,

Till their dark host, in wide array,
Touched with the rising beams of day,
Rich tints of rose and gold display,
And form, as on the sun they wait,
The pomp and triumph of his state.

XIV.

Short triumph here. In cloud of woe
Faded joy's high reflected glow—
At D'Arcy's Earl was aimed the blow.
Fitzharding, quick as glance of light,
The poniard wrenched, with skilful might,
    And laid its ruffian master low.
He, instant, knew the carle he viewed
Was one, who late his steps pursued,
    And watched St. Scytha's shrine.
Not with Fitzharding was his strife;
His aim was at Earl D'Arcy's life;
    But, led by knightly sign,
He traced the Baron on his way;
    The gilded spur upon his heel
    Did shrouded warrior reveal,
And marked him forth for prey.

But, when Fitzharding left his shade,
Hastening to render Florence aid,
The cowl fell back, that veiled his face,
And his pursuer stayed his pace,
Till, guided by strange sounds of joy,
He came the father to destroy.

XV.

Short time had Florence to revive
    From terror and dismay,
Support from tenderness derive,
    Or tender tear repay ;
Short time for speech had sire and son,
Ere the good monk, her guide, came on.
He warmly urged their instant flight ;
    For comrades of the fallen were nigh,—
    Monks, too, who shelter would deny
When they might view this dismal sight.
He would a hidden passage show,
 To serve as screen from menaced woe ;
Till day should send Duke Richard hence,
His march for London to commence,
And all his myrmidons of war,
Guarding their captive King afar.

XVI.

Briefly the Knights their thanks repaid;
   And looked on him, who bore their crest,
All lifeless on the marble laid,—
   Briefly for him their grief expressed:
" Richard Fitzharding—kinsman dear!
On thee will fall the future tear,
When thought may pause upon thy bier !"
Swift on the southern aisle they went
By many a dim-seen monument;
And reached a little shaded door
That led the great west entrance o'er;
Where gallery, that ran between
The crowning battlement, unseen,
Received them in its silent space.
Well knew the Earl this lonely place,
For, even here, at curfew hour,
He refuge sought from Richard's power;
And here remained, till he in vain
Searched for his son among the slain.

XVII.

Oh ! if by care and grief are told
   The unseen steps of Time;

How many hours—nay days—had rolled,
Since, lingering in this secret hold,
　He heard that curfew chime !
Since, on the northern gallery
　His restless steps had strayed,
Where he had viewed, unconsciously,
　His son in monkish shade,
Who there the vision of his face
Amid the shadows seemed to trace.
Now joy told forth the time so fast,
The present moment was the past,
Ere yet he marked it glide along,
Stealing the tale upon his tongue.
Full many an hour had D'Arcy passed,
　Since o'er the NORMAN SHADE
He marked the sun its low beam cast,
　And glow with angry red ;
Since he had heard St. Alban's knell
Sound what had seemed his son's farewell ;
Since from safe nook he turned away,
To seek, where death and danger lay.

XVIII.

Ere now withdrew the monk, their guide,
He bade the warriors here abide
Till morning hour, when they might hear
Drums and the neigh of steeds draw near.
Then, soon as Richard's hosts were gone,
He would return, and lead their way
To chamber, where the Abbot lay.
While grateful words the Knights repay,
Florence could only with a tear
Thank the good priest for service dear.
Time had not yet been lent to tell
The acts, on which she fain would dwell:
The kindness, that restored her life
From grief and horror's mingled strife.
Meekly he bowed his aged head,
And then on soundless foot he sped.
They heard him bar the gallery-door,
And soon, upon the paved floor,
Watched his dark shadow pass away,
Where the high-tombed warriors lay.

XIX.

And now Fitzharding pressed to hear
From Florence all her tale of fear.
She told her sorrows, from the hour
When first she watched St. Alban's tower;
Of her dark path of dread and grief
   Through forest shade; of pilgrim train,
And words exchanged; of wounded chief,
   She feared had been Fitzharding slain.
Told of her courser's sudden flight
Through ruffian-troops fresh from the fight,
His strength, his courage and his speed,
His dexterous course at utmost need;
Till, at St. Alban's warded gate,
Though courage, skill, nor strength abate,
They seized him as a prize of war,
And Florence for their prisoner.
But, ere they led her to close ward,
Her proffered gold to one on guard
Aided her through the barrier,
(Enfolded in her pilgrim-shroud)
Among an anxious, hurrying crowd,

Seeking their friends within the town.
Words might not tell what she had known,
While, by the dying and the dead,
She passed to gain this Abbey's shade;
Nor, when she sunk, beside the bier
Of warrior, laid in chamber near.

xx.

'Twere vain to tell Fitzharding's pain,
While listening to the fearful strain;
How oft he shuddered, oft reproved,
And blamed her most, when most he loved,
For courage rash, for passage won,
And high exploits for his sake done.
Scarce might the Earl his wonder speak,
That one so gentle and so weak
The meed of heroes thus might claim:
But greater fear the less o'ercame.
Then Sire and Son to other tell
What each in yester fight befell;
Of nobles slain, and friends that failed
At utmost need, though horsed and mailed.

But chief their indignation rose
  'Gainst Wentworth—traitor to his king,
  Whose standard basely did he fling
To ground, and fled before his foes!

XXI.

Earl D'Arcy then the story told
  Of many a fugitive he met,
Wounded and lorn, both young and old,
  Seeking a home ere sun was set.
In a close wood near Alban's town,
Laid in a wretched cart, alone,
Sore wounded Dorset, he, with pain,
Saw journeying to his domain—
Him must he never see again!
Stafford's brave Earl on litter borne,
Whose hand by fatal shaft was torn,
Already on his look was laid
Approaching Death's first warning shade.
His gallant father, too, was near,
Who to his tomb the scar would bear
Received this day for Lancaster;
Through vizor closed the arrow sped,
That sent him from his steed as dead,

And nearly had the life-blood quaffed :
Yet fatal was not deemed the shaft.
Ah ! deeply must the shaft of sorrow
Strike to his heart, when, on the morrow,,
He o'er his only son shall stand,
And feel the death-dew on his hand !

XXII.

As this sad image rose to view,
   Earl D'Arcy, as in sympathy,
Gazed on his son, whose living hue
   Awoke his grateful fervency.
A silent tear stood in his eye,
As passed his offered thanks on high.
Well read the son his father's care ;
Rejoiced he in those thanks to share.
But hark ! a low and measured chime
Speaks from the tower the WATCH of PRIME,
Sounding due summons to the knights
For some high pomp of funeral rites.
O'er that west gallery might they bend
And trace nave, choir, from end to end.
The lofty vista, crowned with shade,
On pillars vast was reared,

Where pointed arch, in far arcade,
Mixed with rude Saxon was displayed,
And double tiers above arrayed,
    By superstition feared.
Broad rose the Norman arch on high,
    That propped the central tower,
And forward led the wondering eye
O'er the choir roof's bright canopy,
    To the east window's bower.

XXIII.

How solemn swept before their sight
    This Abbey's inner gloom,
Thwarted with gleams of streaming light
    And shade from pier and tomb,
Flung by lone torch, or by the ray
Of tapers, sickening at the day.
For now, the thunder-clouds o'erpast,
May's crystal morn its dawning cast
On every window's untraced pane,
And touched it with a cold, blue stain.
How peaceful dawned that living light
O'er eyes for ever set in night !

O'er eyes, that, but on yesterday,
Viewed distant years in long array,
And lovely gleams of shaded joy
Upon their evening landscape lie.

XXIV.

In solemn thought, while Sire and Son
    Beheld the fate of friends below,
Their hearts a various feeling own,
    That, saved from every mortal blow,
For them another morning rose,
And brought their wearied limbs repose !
Then Pity shed a tender tear
For many a warrior sleeping here.
And thus, at the first dawn of day,
Their duteous orisons they pay.
The grateful thoughts ascend on high,
Like May's first offerings, to the sky,
That sweet and still and full arise
'Mid silent dews and peaceful sighs ;
Even as the glad lark's soaring trill,
Heard, when the thunder's voice is still,
Rejoicing in the breath of May :—
But, oh ! that sweet and jocund lay

Now yields to other sounds, and dread—
To bell that mourns the slaughtered dead!

XXV.

But see! a sudden radiance streams
  From Alban's choir and shrined tomb;
The sable veil withdrawn, the beams,
  Just kindling, break upon the gloom,
From torch and taper lifted there,
'Mid burnished gold and image fair.
While through the choir the shrine-lights spread,
Gleamed each tall column's branching head,
  Circled with golden blazonry—
The shielded arms of abbots dead.
These shields, so small and close, like gems
Enclasped the columns' clustered stems,
  That rose in the ribbed arch on high,
And spread, in fan-like tracery,
Upon the choir's long canopy;
Where visioned angels shed their light
Upon a vault of mimic night.

XXVI.

And now the long perspective line
  Extending through those arches three,

Of stately grace, above the shrine,
  St. Mary's Chapel they might see,
Distinct, yet stealing from the sight;
  And high, beyond the altar there,
  Her image, shrined in flowers fair,
Lessened afar in softer light,
While, miniatured, before it glide
Her priests, who chaunt at morning-tide.
Again that bell, with solemn tongue,
Through vault and aisle and gallery rung;
Till distant voices, drawing near,
Fell, deeply murmuring, on the ear.
This was the Requiem-mass of Prime,
  The Requiem, sung with honours due,
Of torch and incense, dirge and chime,
  When the whole convent, two and two,
And the Lord Abbot stately led,
In flowing vest, with mitred head—
'Twas the full mass for princes said,
When they repose among the dead.

XXVII.

'Twas then the aged Abbot came,
Obedient to the Monarch's claim.

Beneath the cloister's westward arch,
By the great porch, he held his march,
With all the officers of state,
That on the Abbey's greatness wait.
Of humbler servants twenty-one,
  Bearing before him each a torch,
  Light the high-sweeping Norman porch
With dusky glare, like setting sun,
When yester battle-day was done.
Then paced his monks in double row,
Bearing their hundred tapers, slow,
That beamed upon each bannered saint
And pageant blazoned high and quaint.
The Abbot came with ready zeal,
  Though called from short and needful rest,
  And with pale age and grief oppressed,
To give the Requiem's solemn seal
And passport to a quiet grave;
And weep the tear due to the brave.

XXVIII.

A tear! does Glory claim a tear?
Weeps he upon a Hero's bier?

The maid, as in the tomb she fades;
The youth, once 'tranced in Fancy's shades;
The wedded pair, whose hearts are one,
Who lived each other's world alone;
The infant, that had smiled so fair,
Like cherub, on its mother's care.;
The long-loved parent, sinking slow
Beneath the weight of winter's snow—
O'er these, when in the grave they lie,
May fall the tears from Pity's eye;
But o'er the warrior's tomb should glance
The lightning of a poet's trance.
Cold was the reverend Father's mind,
By wisdom, or by age, refined
To simple truth, that scorns the prize,
For which the bard, the hero, dies—
A shade, a sound, a pageant gay,
A morning cloud of golden May,
Glorious with beams of orient hue,
That, while they flatter—melt it too!
And, for such airy charm, he gives
The real world, in which he lives;

And, gazing on the lofty show,
Sinks in the closing tomb below !—
And therefore fell the Abbot's tear
O'er Glory and a Hero's bier.

XXIX.

While these last rites, from Pity due,
The Abbot gave, you still might view
In his raised eye, the noble mind
That suffered much, yet shone resigned :—
Calm and unbreathing was his look,
As though of all, save soul, forsook ;
And all his form and air conveyed
The aspect of some peaceful shade,
Contented tenant of a cell,
Who long had bade the world farewell.
Still, as he moved, the verse was sung
For crowds of dead they passed among ;
And still the gliding tapers threw
A fleeting, gloomy, livid hue
On every face, on every grave,
Ranged on each side the long wide nave.

Though slaughtered men his pathway bound,
He shrunk not from this dreadful ground.

XXX.

Now, where around dead Somerset
High pomp of funeral-watch was met,
Where o'er his corpse twelve torches blazed,
Circle of light, by almsmen raised,
And choristers beyond attend;
There, slow the Abbey-train ascend,
    And, ranged in triple crescent-rows,
Step above step, the fathers bend,
    While requiem and blessed repose
Are sung, with long-resounding breath,
For all in battle slain, beneath.
How high and full the organs swell,
    And roll along the distant aisle,
Till, dying on the ear, they fell,
    And every earthly thought beguile.
While finely stole the softened strain,
    And stately moved the solemn march,
The Knights and Florence view with pain
    The scene beneath the Norman arch.

Soon as the chaunted hymn was o'er,
PORTCULLIS, on the steps before,
Cried out with lofty voice of dole,
" Say for the soul—say for the soul
Of Somerset, high duke and prince,
And for each soul departed since
The onset of the battle-fray,
The wonted Requiem :—sing and say !"

XXXI.

It was an awful thrilling sight,
Beneath this Abbey's far-drawn flight,
To view her dark-robed sons arranged,
In memory of those thus changed,
Now seen in death laid out below,
Even while the Requiem's tender woe
Did for each parted spirit flow.
And first was seen a mourner pace,
His mantle borne with stately grace,
  His eyes veiled in his hood,
Bearing the princely offering
Of Henry, his sad lord and king,
  Where high the Abbot stood—

The sword of Somerset he bore:
A herald stalked, with casque, before.
He stopped below the Abbot's feet,
With low-bowed head and gesture meet.
Each pious gift the Father took
  With meekest grace and downward eye;
  And gave it to his Prior nigh,
Who held it, with a reverend look,.
  At the bier's head on high.

XXXII.

A second mourner pacing grave,
  Attended by a herald-band,
For the mass-penny offering gave
  An offering for Northumberland.
No pomp appeared, when he bent down,
  Of cushion, or of carpeting;
Such stately signs were given alone
  To greet the Sovereign's offering.
Last, for De Clifford offering came;
And when the herald called his name,
The Abbot, gazing on his bier,
Gave bitter offering of a tear!

And dignified the warrior's grave,
With Virtue's tribute to the brave!
Nearer the aged Father drew,
    Where the chief mourners wait,
And sprinkled there the drops held due
    To Somerset's sad state.
These valued rites alike he paid
To Percy's and De Clifford's shade,
And then, with supplicating eye,
    Stretched forth his hands upon the air,
As if he would a blessing sigh
    On all the dead and living there.

XXXIII.

As sunk the service for the dead,
Deep sighs of grief and mournful dread,
Of pious gratitude and love,
In Florence' gentle bosom strove;
While on his arm she bowed her head,
For whom her thankful tears were shed.
The Knights had watched the sad array,
Till now the rising beams of May

Paled even the torches' yellow flame ;
  And on the vault high overhead,
And on the far perspective, came
  A purer light, a softer shade,
Harmonious, and of deep repose,
Sweet as the Requiem's dying close !
When, sudden, on this calm profound
The war-trump sent its brazen sound.

XXXIV.

Fiercely, though far without the wall,
They heard Duke Richard's trumpet call
The morning-watch, at rising sun.
Then other startling sounds begun,
Voices and drums and trampling hoofs,
  In preparation of their way
  To London with the King this day.
And thus, while all beneath these roofs
Were hushed by hopes Religion lent,
  The brazen shriek of War's fell brood
  Even to the sepulchre pursued
The victims she had thither sent.

Profaning, with a ruthless tongue,
The holy anthem scarcely sung.

XXXV.

Soon as the Requiem was said,
    The Abbot sought the captive King ;
To mourn with him his warriors dead,
    And his last sorrowing farewell bring.
In contemplation deep, and grief,
    Meek Henry watched alone,
Seeking his only sure relief
    Before THE HIGHEST THRONE.
Soon as the Sire drew near, and told
    Names of th' unburied dead,
King Henry felt a withering cold
    O'er all his senses spread :—
Scarce could he thank him for the rite
He had performed this dreadful night ;
For pious courage, that pursued
And that the Victor had subdued,
So far as grant of sepulchre
For those, who thanks could ne'er prefer—'

He would have said,—but utterance failed
To speak for those he now bewailed.

XXXVI.

Yet did he praise the fortitude
That Richard's cruel claims withstood,
And held the rights of sanctuary
For friends o'ercome by misery.
Then for himself he thanked him last,
For hospitable duty past;
For sympathies of look and tone
  While he had been a captive guest;
Such as the broken spirits own,
  And treasure in the grateful breast.
He willed an Anniversary
Should of the fatal yesterday
Be held within this choir, for those,
Whose bodies here find just repose.
He had no treasures left to prove
How much this place deserved his love;
But with meek look he asked, and voice,
  The Abbot would a gift receive,

His only gift—he had no choice—
   The offering would his heart relieve—
Certain rich robes which once he wore,
Fit clothing these for him no more !
Haply such robes might now aspire
To Abbey-use ;—he would desire
That, for his own sake, there should be
A day of Anniversary,
To mark the memory of a friend—
The day when his poor life should end.

XXXVII.

The Abbot bent ; and bowed his head
   To hide the tears that dimmed his eye ;
Faltered the words he would have said—
Of reverence, love, and grief—and fled
   In deep convulsive sigh.
Oh ! had he viewed in future time
The vision of that ghastly crime
(Pointing the pathway to the tomb)
Which marked the day of Henry's doom,
His aged heart at once had failed,
And he had died, while he bewailed.

Henry one moment o'er him hung,
  With look more eloquent than tongue—.
Brief moment of emotion sweet !
Ere the King raised him from his feet :
  But hark ! in Abbey-court there rung
Flourish of trumpets, cheers of crowd,
Shrill steeds and drums all roaring loud.

XXXVIII.

The Abbot rose, but trembled, too;
Yet calm his look of ashy hue.
He sighed, but spoke not.   Steps are heard ;
  A page and knight approach the King ;
  Message from Richard straight they bring,
That all things wait the royal word
For London; and the morning wore.
Faint smile of scorn the King's face bore
At mockery of his princely will,
While captive he to Richard still.
But the meek Henry was not born
To feel, or give, the sting of scorn ;
Soon did that smile in sadness fade,
Tinged soft with resignation's shade—

The paleness of a weeping moon,
Which clouds and vapours rest upon.

XXXIX.

Again the trumpets bray ; again
Ring iron steps, and shouts of men.
In armour cased, Duke Richard came ;
Proudly his warlike form he held, ·
And looked the Spirit of the field,
Yet for King Henry's royal name
Feigned reverence due.   With gentle blame
For lingering thus, he urged him hence,
While mingled o'er his countenance
A milder feeling with his pride—
A pity he had fain denied—
As he that look of goodness viewed,
Beaming in dignity subdued.

XL.

Following his steps came knight and lord,
And filled the royal chamber broad ;
Yet came not Warwick in the throng,
Smitten with consciousness of wrong.

There was in Henry's meekened look
A silent but a deep rebuke,
That smote his heart, and almost drew
His vast ambition from its view.
But, when that look was seen no more,
The pang it caused too soon was o'er,
And rashly his career he held
'Gainst him in council and in field;
And now was with the vanguard gone
To fix the triumph he had won.

XLI.

By the King's side, mourning his fate,
    The aged Abbot stept.
Through chamber, passage, hall, and gate,
Where steeds and squires and lancemen wait,
The Abbey's pomp, the Warrior's
    Their full appointment kept.
When the last portal they had gained,
Close marshalled bands without were trained;
Within, high state the Church maintained.
The Abbot paused, and from his brow
Dismissed the darker cloud of woe,
    To bless his parting Lord;

With arms outstretched, and look serene,
Pity and reverence were seen
   A farewell to afford.
And thus the hundred monks around
  Bestowed their blessings on his head,
While none of all the crowd was found,
  Rude foes, stern soldiers, marshalled,
That did not say, or seem to say,
" Blessings attend thee on thy way !"

XLII.

The farewell Benediction o'er,
Duke Richard willed such scene no more,
And instant signal made to part ;
He scorned, yet feared, each trait of heart.
A smile, a tear, in Henry's eye
Said more than words may e'er supply,
As from the portal slow he past
And turned a long look—and the last.
Loud blew the trumpets, as in scorn
  Of those they left behind
Stretched pale upon these aisles forlorn ;
  Loud blew they in the wind.

The fierce yet melancholy call,
Which died around each sable pall,
Formed but the warrior's wonted knell—
The solemn and the last farewell !

XLIII.

This fearful summons was the last
   That shook the sainted Alban's shrine;
While now the martial pageant past,
   Arrayed in many a glittering line,
From his pale choir and frowning tower,
Sad witness of the battle hour.
And from that broad tower now was seen
Those bands of war, on May's first green,
In gleaming pomp and long array
Winding by meads and woods away;
While Clement viewed them, who, with dread,
Had watched their fires on hill outspread;
Had seen their white tents, dawning slow
On yester-morning's crimsoned brow;
And thought how soon his shrines might fall
Beneath this poorly-battled wall.
He heard their trumpets in the gale

Sink fainter; as they seemed to wail
That Quiet did o'er War prevail.
He heard the tramp of measured tread,
The clattering hoofs, that forward sped;
The numerous voice in sullen hum;
And, last and lone, the hollow drum,
Till far its deadened beat decayed,
   And fell upon the listening ear
Soft as the drop through leafy shade,
   Then trembled into very air.
How still the following pause and sweet,
While yet the air-pulse seemed to beat!

XLIV.

Thus passed the warlike vision by;
While Alban's turrets, peering high
Upon the gold and purpled sky,
O'erlooked the way for many a mile,
And, touched with May-beams, seemed to smile,
—Smile on the flight of War's sad care,
That left them to their sleep in air;
And left the monks of gentle deed,
To blessed thanks from those they speed—

Left the poor friend, who watched his lord
Wounded, unwitting of reward,
To see him to his home restored—
The saintly Abbot left to close
His gathered years in due repose—
The dead unto their honoured tombs;
To peace these aisle's and transept's glooms!

XLV.

When Florence to her home returned
The aged servant she had mourned
    Received her at her gate;
And, pawing on the ground again,
Behold her steed, who prison-rein
Had snapped, and homeward fled amain,
    And here did watchful wait;
And onward to his mistress went,
With playing pace and neck low bent.
Once more beneath her peaceful bower,
  Oh! how may words her feelings tell,
While now she viewed St. Alban's tower,
That, yesterday, even at this hour,
She watched beneath dark Terror's power?—
  One other day had broke his spell!

XLVI.

Farewell ! farewell ! thou Norman Shade !
The waning Moon slants o'er thy head ;
Thy humbler turrets, seen below,
Uplift the darkly-silvered brow,
And point where the broad transepts sweep,
Measuring thy grandeur ; while they keep
In silent state thy watch of night,
Communing with each planet bright ;
And sad and reverendly they stand
Beneath thy look of high command.
Oh ! Shade of ages long gone past,
Though sunk their tumult like the blast,
Still steals its murmur on my ear ;
And, once again, before mine eye,
The long-forgotten scenes sweep by ;
Called from their trance, though hearsed in Time,
   Bursting their shroud, thy forms appear,
With darkened step and front sublime,
   Sadness, that weeps not—strength severe.
And still, in solemn ecstasy,
I hear afar thy Requiem die ;

Voices harmonious through thy roofs aspire,
The high-souled organ breathes a seraph's fire !
Peace be with all beneath thy presence laid :
Peace and farewell !—farewell, thou Norman Shade !

END OF ST. ALBAN'S ABBEY.

NOTES.

NOTES.

Bold is this Abbey's front, and plain.—vol. iii. p. 95.

ALTHOUGH the history of the Abbey, in and near which the scenes of this poem are laid, has been given in several well-known publications, it will, perhaps, not be unacceptable to any reader to have a few dates and other particulars respecting it, brought to his recollection.

The Abbey was founded in the year 793, by Offa, second king of Mercia of that name ; whose power was acknowledged in twenty-three provinces, or districts, which are said to have been co-extensive with the same number of the shires, into which Alfred afterwards divided England.

The spot, on which St. Alban, the first English martyr, suffered, is supposed to be that, on which the Abbey-church stands ; his bones having been there found. The hill was then woody ; and its

name (Holmhurst) would seem to imply also, that
it was once, if not entirely in the midst of water, so
nearly surrounded by streams, as to be considered
insular. Materials for the earlier parts of the Monastery and Church were found in the ruins of the
city, which the Romans called Verulamium, or Vero-
lamium, from the British name for the stream, which
still flows in the meads below. In many parts of
the exterior walls of the church Roman bricks may
be easily traced; and, about twenty years since,
small fragments of these materials, readily known
by the fineness and bright redness of the baked
earth, were, not uncommonly, found in the meadow
on the south-western side of the Church, formerly
the site of the cloisters.

The Church exhibits the styles of architecture of
several ages, " from earliest Saxon down to that of
the Tudor construction." Mr. Carter, in his " Plan
and Account of the North side of the Nave," allots
to the Thirteenth Century the first four divisions
(arches) from the West, which are of the Pointed
order; the next nine divisions (arches with three
sweeps—mouldings) are of the Saxon order; as are
the great piers and arches of the Tower, rising
nearly to the height of the Nave,—just above which
is the gallery, that runs all round the Tower; then
follow, in perspective, the five grand arches of the

Choir and Saint's Chapel, apparently of the fifteenth century, more pointed and lofty than the first four arches. On the south side of the Nave, the Pointed order includes ten arches from west to east; the style then becomes Saxon to the great east pillar of the Tower, which stands far in the Choir; and then follow five arches of the Pointed order and of the fifteenth century, answering to those on the north side.

That part, which Mr. Carter calls Saxon, the previous " Observations" call Norman of the style of Henry I.; but there are several undisputed remains of the Saxon edifice. The eastern arches of the Nave are round, with three mouldings; and their pillars, massive and irregular, are of rubble-work of Roman bricks, covered with Saxon plaster.

Other pillars, next in date, of the Nave, were built by Abbot Paul, a Norman, the first abbot appointed by William the Conqueror. In one of these is a staircase, the door of which is now filled up, communicating with the galleries all round. These galleries thread the walls. The small arches in the second story of the centre tower light a gallery of communication to each side of that tower. Besides the galleries here mentioned, was one, which ran behind the open-work of the great screen from side to side of the Choir. By a note in p. 399 of the

Rev. Mr. Newcomb's ample History of the Abbey, it appears, that this screen, which has been by some attributed to Wallingford, and by others to Whethamstede, was probably designed by the former, whose arms appear upon it, and completed by the latter. It cost 1100 marks, and is of the richest Gothic style. A large curtain of crimson velvet, or of gold tissue, was sometimes suspended on it.

Whethamstede was abbot, on his re-election, at the time of the first battle of St. Alban's. After the battle, he begged of the Duke of York the dead bodies of the Duke of Somerset and others, for interment: none having dared to touch them, while they were lying in the streets.

Of the high vaulted porch beneath.—p. 96.

This beautiful porch is of the style of the time of Henry the Third. The richly-carved oaken doors within, Mr. Gough says, are of the fifteenth century.

Here forty abbots have ruled and one.—p. 97.

Carter reckoned forty Abbots of St. Alban's; Willis and Newcomb forty-one:—the latter estimate includes the second presidency of Whethamstede, who was re-elected, after an interval of more than twenty years, having resigned in 1440.

Freed from Peter's pence were they.—p. 97.

Weaver says of this and the other privileges of the Abbey,—" Before the Dissolution, such were the privileges of this place, that the King could make no secular officer over them, but by their owne consent; they were alone quite from paying that Apostolical custome and rent, which was called Romscot, or Peter-pence; whereas, neither King, Archbishop, Bishop, Abbot, Prior, nor any one in the kingdome, was freed from the payment thereof. The Abbot also, (or Monke appointed Archdeacon under him) had pontifical jurisdiction over all the priests and laymen, of all the possessions belonging to this Church, so as he yielded subjection to no Archbishop, Bishop, or Legate, save onely to the Pope of Rome. This Abbot had the fourth place among the Abbots, which sate as Barons in the Parliament house. Howsoever, Pope Adrian the Fourth, whose surname was Breakespeare, born hereby at Abbots-Langley, granted this indulgence to the Abbots of this Monasterie: that, as St. Alban was distinctly knowne to be the first Martyr of the English nation: so the Abbot of this Monasterie should at all times among other Abbots of England, in degree of dignitie, be reputed first and principall. The Abbot and Covent of this house were acquitted of

all toll through England. They made Justices *ad
audiendum et terminandum,* within themselves ; and
no other Justice could call them for any matter out
of their libertie. They made Bayliffes and Coro-
ners ; they had the execution and returne of all
writs, the goods of all outlawes, with gaole and
gaole deliverie within themselves. .... This
Abbey was surrendered up by the Abbot and
Monkes there ; by delivering the Covent seale into
the hands of T. Pope, D. Peter, Master Caven-
dish, and other the King's visitors, the fifth day of
December, 1539. It was valued, at a farre under
rate, to bee worth of yearely revenue, two thousand
five hundred and ten pounds, sixe shillings, penny-
halfpenny."

Kings and heroes here were guests.—p. 98.

In the prosperous days of the Abbey, several
apartments were built exclusively for the use of
strangers. These adjoined the Cloisters. Beyond
them, in a separate range of buildings, were the
King's and Queen's apartments. Notwithstanding
this preparation for visitors and these indirect invi-
tations, it seems from Matthew Paris, that some of
the earlier Kings came too often, or, at least, with
too cumbrous suites. In still earlier times, for the
purpose of lessening these visits, an expensive pur-

chase had been made, of a temptation, which had too
frequently drawn the Courts into this neighbour-
hood. Ælfric, the seventh Abbot, bought of the King,
probably Edgar, *the great fishpool;* " for," says Mr.
Newcomb, from M. Paris, " it was a fishery belonging to the King, whose house, or palace, was that
now called Kingsbury; and this pool, by reason of its
vicinity to the Abbey, and the pride of the royal
servants, had been hurtful and troublesome to the
religious body. Ælfric, therefore, in order to prevent
the like inconvenience, cut a passage through the
head which banked up the waters, and, draining
them off, turned it all into dry land ; preserving only
a small pool for the use of the Abbey. And M.
Paris, who wrote about 1240, says, ' To this day are
to be seen the banks and shores of the great lake,
adjoining to the way which leads westward, and is
called Fishpool-street. The rest of the drained land
was turned into gardens."

It is one of the circumstances, which render the
town of St. Alban's so rich in antiquarian memorials
and localities, that *Fishpool Street* still bears its ancient denomination, and is thus, at this day, a record of a transaction, which dates from the tenth
century. Whoever will take the trouble of going
upon the leads of the Abbey will also perceive in the
state, or shape, of the land adjoining the road from

St. Alban's to Hatfield, some symptoms of the
" banks and shores," which Matthew Paris speaks
of as visible in his time.   At least, these symptoms
were perceivable about twenty years since.

But now, nor dais, nor halls remain.—p. 98.

The *dais*, or *deis*, was the high table, which ran
athwart the upper end of halls in palaces and noble
mansions, in some of which, and in college-halls, it
remains at this day.   It was frequently raised so
high, that the approach to it was by two or three
successive flights of steps, at the top of each of
which the servants, bringing up dishes, were allowed
to wait while some appointed verse was sung.
Chaucer, describing the festivities of the Tartarian
King, Cambuscan, on his birth-day, says that the
King

> " In real vestiments sit on his deies,
>   With diademe, ful high in his paleis,
>   And holt his feste so solempne and so riche,
>   That, in this world, ne was ther none it liche."
>   *The Squire's Tale.*

Gawin Douglas, in his version of the Æneid, says
of Dido at the feast, " The Queene was set at deis."
What Matthew Paris says on this subject may be
rendered, " The Prior dining at the great table,
which is generally called *deis :*" and again, " A cup

with a foot is not allowed in the Refectory, except
at the great table, which we call *deis.*" The word
occurs frequently in our older writers. It sometimes meant the cloth of state placed on the high
table; sometimes a canopy: Dr. Percy seems to
think the latter its original meaning.

Spoke doom to all his vassal throng.—p. 101.

The civil privileges and power of the Abbey,
which were always great, were confirmed and extended by a charter of Edward IV. in poor compen-
sation of the losses it sustained during the civil
wars. This power was exercised in the towns of
St. Alban's, Watford and Barnet, which were the
towns of the Abbey, in the hundred of Cashio, and
in a considerable space round St. Alban's, called its
liberty. That the Abbey lands extended anciently
far to the south appears from the punishment,
inflicted by William the Conqueror, who, in revenge
for the warlike resistance made to him by Abbot
Frederick, the Saxon, called Frederick the Bold,
despoiled the Abbey of all lands *lying between
Barnet and London.* Over the north gate of the
Abbey, which led into the grand court, was the
temporal prison for those judged by the Abbot; a
building still used as the town gaol. It may, indeed,
be supposed to have been used by several of the

Abbots, as a place of punishment for the towns-
people, who frequently rose against the power of the
Abbey, and even besieged, during ten days together,
the great gate of the Convent in Holywell-street,
of which there are not now any remains. This was
in the time of Abbot Hugo de Evetsden, about the
year 1326. It was about six in the evening of
January 21st, that the townsmen, some on foot and
some on horse, began to assault the gate, not only
with great tumult, but by setting fire to it. The
fire does not appear, however, to have done much
damage. The Abbot had foreseen this outrage, and
had prepared for defence, by summoning to the
Convent 200 of his dependants, who, with courage,
long watchings and much fasting (for they were ill-
provided for a siege), kept the enemy at bay till the
King sent an order to the Sheriff, who read a proclamation to the assailants, and dispersed them.
They urged, in their defence, that the Abbot had
acted in an arbitrary manner, relative to some privileges, which, they thought, remained to them. To
prove this they appealed to Domesday-book. In reply, the Abbot's council produced a grant, by which
Henry II. granted to the church of St. Alban's "the
Vill of St. Alban, with every liberty, or privilege
which borough ought to have." Notwithstanding
this, the Abbot, by command of King Edward the

Second, and to procure tranquillity, afterwards signed
a grant of privileges, against which the Archdeacon
and all the monks protested. This grant, however,
they afterwards signed, in awe of the King; and it
probably continued in force till Edward VI. in-
corporated the town in the year 1553. For further
particulars see Newcomb's History of St. Alban's.

For here the Pilgrim's Lodge arose.—p. 103.

" Abbot Geoffry de Gonham built a large and
noble hall, with a double roof, to entertain strangers
in, near which he built a fair bed-chamber," says
Willis. But Abbot John of Hertford did more ; he
raised *chimneys.* " He built a noble hall for the
use of strangers, adding many parlours, with an inner chamber *and a chimney,* and a noble picture, and
an entry, and a small hall ; and a most noble entry,
with a porch, or gallery, and many fair bedcham-
bers, with their inner chambers and chimneys, to receive strangers honourably."—Willis's Mitred Abbies.

There the Scriptorium spread its gloom.—p. 104.

Every great abbey had a room where the monks,
and sometimes other persons not members of the
community, copied and illuminated ancient manu-
scripts, and transcribed service-books for the choir.
In some abbeys one side of the great cloister was

inclosed for a Scriptorium, as at Gloucester, where
the whole south side of the fine cloister was so ap-
propriated. The monks learned and practised not
only the art of illuminating books, but several other
ornamental arts, by the exercise of which they deco-
rated their churches and convents. The porcelain
tiles, for pavement of the high altar, were frequently prepared by them, as were the fresco-paint-
ings on the walls of chapels and cloisters. Of their
performance were also the armorial bearings pencilled on windows and tombs, with scroll work and
" painted imagery," such as, Weaver says, Abbot
John of Whethamstede " dressed up" this his
Monastery of St. Alban withal. That monks made
their own gloves appears by a grant, which Charle-
magne delivered to those of St. Sithin, about the
year 790, " of unlimited right of hunting, for
making their own gloves and girdles of the skins of
the deer then killed, and covers for their books."
See Warton's History of English Poetry.--The Scriptorium of St. Alban's was built about the year 1080,
by Abbot Paul, or Paulin, a Norman, who had many
volumes transcribed there, from copies lent by Archbishop Lanfranc, his countryman, whose influence
with William the Conqueror had saved this Abbey
from destruction. Warton says that more than
eighty books were transcribed at St. Alban's, by

order of Whethamstede, who, he adds, died about
1440; an error into which he was led by Weaver,
who was himself probably deceived by the circumstance of that abbot having resigned his office
about that time, and having become a private monk
of the convent; influenced, perhaps, by the storm
which he saw impending over his friend and patron,
Duke Humphrey. On the death of his successor,
John Stoke, Whethamstede was re-elected abbot,
in the year 1451; which rank he held till his death,
in 1464, as is proved by a book in the library of the
Heralds' College, mentioned by Willis, and entitled
" Regist. Rob: Blakeney Capellan: Dom: Ramridge." The fine fretted tomb, or rather shrine, of
Abbot Ramridge, is near the altar on the right, and
opposite to that of Whethamstede; the ram's head,
in allusion to his name, appearing among the ornaments of the cornices, as do wheatsheafs on the
plainer and less elegant altar-tomb of the latter abbot, which he had constructed in his life-time, at an
expense, as is recorded, of more than seventy-four
pounds.

Round blessed Mary in her bower.—p. 104.

In a note to his " Travels in the Holy Land," Dr.
Clarke gives the following interesting explanation
of the custom of surrounding illuminated pictures

of the Virgin and other sacred representations, with lilies and wreaths of flowers. These were chosen not merely as embellishments, but as allusions to the city, the earthly residence of our SAVIOUR; the word Nazareth signifying, in Hebrew, a flower. " Hence the cause, wherefore, in ancient paintings used for illuminating missals, the rose and the lily, separately or combined, accompany pictures of the Virgin. In old engravings, particularly those of Albert Durer, the Virgin is rarely represented unaccompanied by the lily."—vol. ii. p. 411. first edit.

Him, whose small pencil thus enshrined.—p. 105.

Allan Strayder, an illuminator of this abbey, painted, in the Golden Register here, portraits of all the principal benefactors of the Abbey. He is also himself mentioned as a benefactor, " for that he forgave three shillings and fourpence of an old debt, owing to him for colours." See Weaver's Funeral Monuments. The art of painting on vellum was of high antiquity in England. The most splendid ornaments and delicately miniatured scenes from scripture were painted on missals, and sometimes portraits of the owner, or of the person, to whom he designed to present the book. Translations from the classics and chronicles were also, in later times, thus ornamented. Duke Humphrey of Gloucester presented to the library of the Divinity-school at

Oxford, several finely-illuminated MSS. and some to this Abbey of St. Alban's. But the most exquisite illuminators were the Florentines; and the most celebrated of these was Giulio Clovio, who thus ornamented the "Missal of Rafaelle," now at Strawberry Hill. See Anecdotes of the Arts in England.

That stretched to learning a preserving hand.—
p. 105.

This Abbey was the second in England in which the press was used:—that of Westminster is well known to have been the first. One of the earliest works printed at St. Alban's was the book on hawking and hunting, translated by Juliana Berners, prioress of the Nunnery of Sopewell, a neighbouring cell of this abbey. She was a sister of Lord Berners, who fought in the first battle here. The first book known to have been printed at St. Alban's, bears date 1480; that of Juliana Berners, 1486. But Caxton, who brought printing into England, and who practised the art in the Abbey at Westminster, about the year 1471, had types much superior to those used at St. Alban's. The cessation of printing here is imputed to the power of Wolsey, who had been Abbot of St. Alban's, and who is said to have expressed, in a convocation in the Chapter-house of St. Paul's, his disapprobation of the press, and his fear of its effects upon the interests of the Romish Church.

The Royal lodging's stately pile.—p. 106.

The Royal apartments were separated by a long cloister-walk from the rest of the monastery. They extended on the brow, that overlooked the valley of the Ver. In the plan of the Royal lodgings still extant are specified the Queen's parlour and her chamber, the Audience Chamber, the King's parlour, considerably larger than the other rooms, and the Refectory. The chief part of the monastery was between this range of buildings and the Abbey-Church. See in Newcomb's History, a plan of the Monastery, as it existed in the time of Henry III.

Kings seemed their Windsor's groves to view.—p. 106.

It has been often supposed that the Gothic aisle was, at first, an imitation of a superb avenue of trees, or, at least, that the architect of the edifice had the idea of it suggested to him by the effect of that fine arrangement of natural productions. Of this theory the best illustration that can, perhaps, be found in England, is afforded by an avenue of elms and limes, called King Charles's Walk, in the Lower Park at Windsor. The trees are so planted as to give a very striking representation of a Pointed Gothic window, with its mullions and Gothic tracery; but the resemblance is not perfect till you have advanced a considerable way down the linden part of the avenue.

His Lodge and Cloister of repose.—p. 108.

The Abbot's cloister lay within the angle of the upper south aisle and the transept. There appears to have been a private door of communication between this cloister and that aisle, which probably was the abbot's way to the choir, when he did not go in the procession of the monks, on days of festival. This door is opposite to one leading into the chancel, near the altar, and close beside the Abbot's seat in the choir; a situation corresponding to that where the Bishop's throne is now placed in a Cathedral. Over that door is an ancient painting of skeletons; meant, perhaps, as a monitory record to the living abbot of his departed brethren laid in the choir."

He sat at the high dais, like prince, alone.—p. 110.

In Gough's British Topography, vol. i. p. 462, is a note containing some particulars of a very curious paper in the hand-writing of Mr. Ashmole, respecting some customs of the Abbey of St. Alban's. A Mr. Robert Shrimpton, who had been mayor of

the town four times, and who lived to the age of
103, remembered the Abbey before the Dissolution ;
and would often discourse of the manners of the
monastery and of the ceremonies and grand processions. He related that " in the great hall was an
ascent of fifteen steps to the abbot's table, to which
the monks brought up the service, in plate, staying
at every fifth step, which was a landing place, to
sing a short hymn. The abbot usually sat alone at
the middle of the table. When a nobleman, or am-
bassador, or stranger of eminent quality came thither, he sat, indeed, at the abbot's table, but it was
towards the lower end. After the monks had
waited awhile on the abbot, they sat down at two
other tables, placed at the other sides of the hall,
and had their service brought in by the novices,
who, when the monks had dined, sat down to their
own dinner. In the Abbey was a large room, having
beds set on each side, for the receiving strangers and
pilgrims, where they had lodging and diet for three
days, without question made from whence they
came." Mr. Nichols, in the 6th Volume of his
Literary Anecdotes, says " It was at one time
Mr. Gough's wish, that his remains should be placed
in the tomb of Whethamstede, abbot of St. Alban's." This was an exquisite trait of an antiquary,
who published the most splendid work, that ever

appeared on the Sepulchral Monuments of Great Britain.

The raised platform, supporting the high table, which ran athwart the sides of great halls, is supposed to have been of-eastern origin, and to have been adopted in England about the time of the wars in the Holy Land, together with the small panelled wainscot containing little cupboards, and the latticed windows near the roof. The suspension of armorial bearings and of instruments of the chace, on the walls of such chambers, is also an Oriental custom. In such a hall, it may be recollected, Dr. Clarke was received at Turkmanlé on his journey from the plain of Troy. See Clarke's Travels, vol. ii. p. 125.

The Abbey's noble Seneschal.—p. 110.

Sir Richard Hastings, afterwards Lord Hastings, was, in the time of Richard III. Seneschal of this Abbey. His office included that of Hundredor, or Judge of the Hundred Courts, with that of Steward of the Abbey, who had the care of its estates. The Abbot, when he received from Henry I. the original grant (which Edward IV. renewed) of the hundred of Cashio, received, in fact, privileges and authorities, which invested him with a degree of royal power. He appointed a Hundredor, or Seneschal, and confirmed the office by patent under the Abbey seal. The Court of the Hundred was held in that great Gate of the Abbey, which now remains. There, causes even of life and death were decided in after-times. The office of Equerry, or Marshal, of the Abbey, was also granted by patent under its seal.

There was the Prior's delegated sway.—p. 110.

This Abbey had a Prior and two Sub-Priors, one of the latter of whom, assisted by three monks, was appointed to serve only at the shrine of the Martyr Amphibalus, the friend and tutor of St. Alban. Thomas..... whose figure in brass, small, but fine and still perfect, lies in the choir, though not over his grave, was once a Sub-prior here.

But all in copes most costly and most gay.—p. 111.

In the time of Whethamstede many of the ancient rules of the monastery, which had been disused, were revived; among these is an order, " that the monks and officiating person should be clothed, for the greater solemnity, in the most costly and splendid garments," on great festivals. (Newcomb.)— There was also an order, directing that the younger monks, who should proceed with wax-lights before the Abbot, should walk upright and with regularity.

There every trencher he assays.—p. 113.

" When the Marshall and the Sewer, with his dish, had gone up the hall, and had made obeisance, on approaching the dais, the Sewer bent beside the Carver, who received and uncovered every dish as it came, and, dipping a *cornet of trencher bread* into each, gave it to the Sewer and to the bearer of the dish to taste." Leland Coll.

With due form and good countenance.—p. 114.

The Chaplain is directed to take up the Alms-Dish, with " a good countenance," and deliver it to the Almoner.

Marched the huge Wassail-bowl the last.—p. 115.

Matthew Paris says, that the Wassail-bowl, in great monasteries, was placed on the abbot's table, at the upper end of the Refectory, or eating-hall, to be circulated among the community at his direction. It was called the *Poculum Caritatis,* and was filled with wine, which, if sweetened and spiced, was called Hypocras. Sometimes it contained the humbler potion of Metheglin, or Mead. This Wassail-bowl came only on extraordinary occasions. The " Forme of Cury" contains a list of the ingredients of Hypocras.

Here, with proud grace, did Wolsey stand.—p. 116.

Wolsey retained this Abbey after he was made archbishop of York and a cardinal.

When Give-Ale and the Dole were o'er.—p. 117.

The Give-Ale, so called, was distributed on anniversaries, often with bread and other Dole for the poor, for which purpose land had been left to the church by the person whose birth-day, or Saint's day, or burial-day, was to be commemorated. Anniversaries were sometimes kept on the birth-day of a donor, during his life-time, or on the Saint's day of the church where it was appointed. The doles of money and bread were distributed at some altar in the church, or at the tomb of a deceased benefactor. The Give-Ale, being chiefly allotted to great festivals, was usually distributed in the church-porch, where the people assembled; who sometimes remained wassailing in the church-yard till it became a scene of merriment and tumult. Some of these anniversaries, as it is well known, gave rise to Fairs, which were once most improperly held in church-yards.

Here, too, the Minstrels' chaunted song.—p. 117.

Minstrels were not only received into monasteries, and paid for their performances, but the monks sometimes wrote lays and ballads for them. Warton, in his History of English Poetry, mentions six minstrels from Buckingham, who were paid four shillings by the treasurer of the priory of Bicester, in Oxfordshire, for singing a legend in the refectory. It was customary for the regular minstrels of the nobility to attend, on festivals, at the neighbouring monasteries, and to be well rewarded on such occasions. Even when minstrels came in the retinue of their lords, they were paid by the monks for their performances. Some great monasteries maintained minstrels of their own. Jeffrey, the harper, in the reign of Henry II., received an annuity from Hyde Abbey, near Winchester; and the Abbies of Conway and Stratflur, in Wales, each maintained a bard, says Warton, who adds, that the Welsh monasteries, in general, were the grand repositories of the poetry of the British bards. At the installation-feast of Abbot Ralp, of St. Augustine's Monastery, in Canterbury, twenty shillings were given to minstrels, who sang to their harps; while six thousand guests were entertained in and about the hall of the monastery.

With tales of Chivalry's high state.—p. 117.

The monks were fond of tales of chivalry and of metrical romances, with which their libraries abounded; and sometimes they turned prose histories into verse, to be sung by minstrels; or, if moulded into a dramatic form, to be represented by themselves. Even the story of Robin Hood was not unfrequently exhibited to the people on days of festival. In an ancient church-account of St. Helen's in Abingdon, is a charge of eighteen pence for setting up " Robinhood's Bower," and another of one shilling for " two dossin of motrin belles." But these indecorous practices, and others still more blameable—the profane and even burlesque representations, for instance, which were permitted during the processions of the boy-bishop—resulted from the Roman Catholic policy of indulging the people in every gratification, which, being connected with the Romish authority, might attach them to it.

Where the raised platform, near the Bay.—p. 120.

The projecting window which, when it occurred over a portico, was called an oriel, was called a Bay window when it opened at an end of the Dais, in a hall, or state-chamber; and then the space

near it was called the Bay. But in this latter situation it was usually much larger than in the
former. Whether its name arose from the shelter
it afforded to the servants and side-boards, or from
the circumstance of its having that degree of extent
which in old buildings was called a *bay*, let better
antiquaries determine. That the word once meant
a certain portion of space in buildings, and was used
as a term of measurement by builders, may be seen
in various old descriptions of houses, which are
there not said to be of so many feet in extent, but
of so many *bays*.

'Mid roial glass and fretwork small.—p. 120.

" Royal glass ;"—painted windows are so called
in ancient poetry.

> " In her oryall, where she was
> .Closed with royall glas
> Fulfylled yt was with ymagery."
> The old romance of *The Squire of Low Degree.*

In front, the velvet curtain, flung.—p. 120.

It was Abbot John of Whethamstede, who re-
mitted to Lord Hastings forty pounds of a desperate
debt for a very rich and curious set of hangings,
used only on days of solemnity; and which had
adorned the great chamber of that nobleman's mansion, near the monastery, during the summer months
only.

Leisurely read the rare Lent Book.—p. 122.

Among the laws given by Archbishop Lanfranc, in the year 1072, to the monks of England, is an injunction that, at the beginning of Lent, the librarian of each convent shall give to every member of it a book to be read in the course of the year, and returned at the following Lent, on pain of humiliation before his superior, and supplication for indulgence.—See Warton.

In leonine, of Latin quaint.—p. 122.

Pasquier (Recherches de la France, p. 596,) traces the origin of rhymed Latin verse no farther back than to Leoninus, or Leonius, once a monk of St. Victor, (at Marseilles) who wrote in Paris, during the reign of Louis VII, about the year 1154. The fashion of using this perversion of the true rhythmus became such, about that time, that, says Pasquier, those who *poetised* (*poetisoient*) in Latin, thought their verses not praiseworthy unless they were rhymed. But Warton clearly shows that the practice should be dated much higher. He had seen a poem of four hundred lines of rhyming Latin, written in the time of Justinian II., in the year 707. Some think that Pope Leo II, who made many alterations in the chaunts of the church, was the inventor of this sort of verse, about the year 1680.

From sainted Oswyn's shrine and tomb.—p. 123.

St. Oswyn's altar stood in the nave, near St. Cuthbert's screen.

Of the good Abbot Delamere.—p. 123.

Delamere, a Norman, and Prior of Tynemouth, was made Abbot of St. Alban's in the year 1349, succeeding Abbot de Mentmore, who had died of the plague, being the first of forty-eight members of the house, who, in that year, died of the same disease. He was a man of a more informed mind and more elegant taste than many of the abbots of St. Alban's, if we may judge from the rules he introduced into his convent, and the style of his ornamental improvements there. A chantry-chapel, built in memory of him, was in a recess of the south transept; but his figure, very finely engraved on a plate of brass, ten feet long, lies over his grave in the chancel, very near the altar-steps; and is, perhaps, the most beautiful and perfect monumental brass remaining in England.

The good Duke Humphrey's mouldering form.—p. 123.

The magnificent tomb, or rather shrine, of Duke Humphrey, is still adorned with seventeen small figures of kings in brass, each in his niche. Other statues, of a larger size, once stood on the opposite side of the tomb. These were probably destroyed by the republican soldiers, whom Cromwell atro-.ciously quartered in the church, and whose horses stood in the aisles.

In a manuscript, dated 1450, is an account of the cost of this tomb, and of the yearly expenses for services performed there. " The Abbot and convent of the said monasterye have paid for makyng the tumbe and sepulture of the said duke, within the said monasterye, above the sum of 433l. 6s. 8d." The Abbot and Prior, for attending there on the day of his anniversary only, received a stipend of 10l. each. For their attendance on that day also, forty monks, priests, received yearly 3s. 8d. each; and one hundred and twenty-two monks, not priests, 3s. 4d. each. Thirteen poor men, who held torches round the shrine on that occasion, had each 2s. 2d. Money was distributed to the poor in the churches of St. Peter's and St. Michael's pa-rishes. The yearly charge for torches and other wax, burned occasionally, is 6l. 13s. 4d. The lands, left by Duke Humphrey to defray these charges, were also to furnish sixty pounds yearly for the kitchen of the abbey, " in relief of the grete decay of livehode of the said monastery in the marches

of Scotland, which beforetime hath be appointed to
the said kechyn." The priory of Tynemouth, among
other far-stretched lands, belonged to the Abbey of
St. Alban's.

The image of a stately Queen.—p. 124.

Margaret of Anjou was heavily suspected of having conspired with Beaufort and Suffolk, in the
death of Duke Humphrey. It is too certain, that
her unprincipled and short-sighted policy led her
to violate the promise of pardon and life, made by
her husband to the Lord Bonvil and Sir Thomas
Kiriel; who, in reliance upon it, had remained
with him in his tent, after they had lost the battle,
and the other confederated lords had fled.

The sacred temple still endures.—p. 129.

When the abbey lands were seized, the monastery of St. Alban's levelled with the ground and
the materials sold, the church would have shared
the same fate, had not the Corporation of the town
purchased it, for about 400*l.*

Glanced on the Abbey-knight beside.—p. 138.

This abbey had six Knights, to whom a certain
portion of the abbey-land was assigned, on condition

of their attendance, at the abbey, in times of any
danger. They were also the body-guard of the
Abbot on journeys, finding their own horses and
arms, but travelling at the expense of the convent.
Abbot William of Trumpington first required the
attendance of these knights in travelling, during a
journey which he made, in the reign of Henry III.
to the priory of Tynemouth. At that time, this
was not merely a matter of pomp :—bands of rob-
bers then infested the highways, and lurked within
the numerous forests of the kingdom; government
was so weakly administered that disorders of every
kind were committed. Military retinues became
general with all, who could support them, and the
necessity, after ceasing to be real, still operated
as a pretence, whenever ambition, or pride, chose to
employ it. The powerful nobles came to the king's
councils, with little armies of retainers; Cardinal
Wolsey, when he last went from London to York,
travelled with a train of one hundred and sixty horse.

Watched where the far-off signals blaze.—p. 139.

The Greeks used torches for signals, and expressed
the approach of friends, or enemies, by the manner
in which they showed them, tossing them for an
enemy, and holding them still for friends. See the

Archæologia, vol. i. where Æschylus is referred to,
as telling, that torches were likewise made to ex-
press a more particular meaning—Clytemnestra
professing to have had the capture of Troy announ-
ced to her by lights, exhibited, according to the or-
ders of Agamemnon, for her information, at Mycenæ;
but it seems, that a commentator considers this as
a mere possibility, to be accounted for only by the
supposition that the lights were displayed on
Mount Ida, and seen from Mount Athos.

And Gorhambury's turrets pale.—p. 139.

The manor of Gorhambury belonged to the Abbey of St. Alban's, being part of their lands at
Westwick. Abbot Geoffry de Gorham, who built
a hall there, granted it probably as a leasehold to a
relative of his own, from whom it received it's name
and to whom the grant was confirmed by a succeeding Abbot, also a relative. Having been given by
Henry VIII. at the Dissolution, to Sir Ralph Raw-
lett, it was sold by him to the Lord Keeper Bacon,
from whom it descended to his celebrated son.

Of studded gates, that, in old wars.—p. 142.

In wars, or, at least, violent contentions with the
townsmen. The massive studded gates of the great

Gate-house, which led into the largest court of the
Abbey, may still be seen under that noble archway ;
but the chief entrance to the monastery was from
Holywell-street, nearly opposite to Sopewell-lane,
of which, however, there are not now any traces on
the spot, houses having been built upon its site.

Though, as they flashed from Julian's wood.—p. 154.

St. Julian's was a cell of the Abbey of St. Alban's, as was likewise the Priory of Sopewell ; of
which latter house the Duchess of Clarence, widow
of the brother of Henry V. had been prioress.

Portcullis-bars in gold were there.—p. 161.

The gold portcullis was a device taken by the
first Duke of Somerset, John de Beaufort, in the
year 1443, from his ancestor, John of Gaunt. Of
this device Henry VII. was afterwards sufficiently
jealous and ostentatious. Somerset's Pouruivant
was called Portcullis.

By royal Banner-knights a throng.—p. 162.

" In the time of the fourth Edward, the allowance in his court for a Knight Bannerett, with
twenty-four servants, was two hundred pounds
a year; for a Knight of the Household, with six-

teen servants, one hundred."—Royal Household Book.

Of Edmund Westby, th' Hundredor.—p. 167.

Edmund Westby, the Hundredor of St. Alban's, whose house, in Peter-street, the king made his head-quarters during the battle. The royal standard was planted before this house, on the Green, which was then called Ouselowe, and sometimes Sandforth, in Peter-street.

And this was Lancaster's reply.—p. 172.

Stowe (edit. 1592) gives the following as the king's reply :—

"I King Henry charge and commaunde, that no manner person, of what degree, estate, or condition soever hee bee, abide not, but they avoide the fielde, and not bee so hardie to make resistaunce against mee in mie owne realme. For I shall knowe what traitour dare be so boulde to arise anie people in mine owne lande, where through I am in great disease and heavinesse : by that faith I owe unto St. Edwarde, and unto the Crowne of Englande, I shall destroie them, everie mother sonne..........
in example, to make all sich traytours to beware for to make anie rising of people within mine owne

lande, and so trayterously to abide their king and governour. And for a conclusion, rather than they shall have anie lorde that here is with mee, at this time, I shall this daie, for their sake, in this quarrell myselfe live and die." p. 650:

Raising he treacherous onset-call.—p. 174.

The first battle of St. Alban's and the first of that long series of battles between the houses of York and Lancaster, which desolated so many families, began between eleven and twelve at noon, on Thursday the 22d of May, 1455. An epitaph, copied by Weaver from a grave-stone in St. Peter's Church, seems to settle the disputed date of this battle. It is on Ralph Babworth, an Esquire of Henry the Sixth's, and on his son, a Sewer to that king, who both fell in this first battle; and runs thus, " the last day of their light was the twentith two of May."

The Knight, who flew to Richard's need.—p. 180.

" He broke in on the garden-side, with a great cry of ' A Warwick! a Warwick,' shouted around him: 'Twas marvel to hear," says Stowe. This garden-side, as it was called, ran along Sopewell-lane, and seems to have been part of the ground belonging to the late Dowager Countess Spencer.

Key's Field, on which Richard Duke of York encamped, ran along the opposite side of the lane, and spread beyond Holywell-street. A narrow slip of it still bears the old name. In Sopewell-lane Somerset was killed; it was the barrier there, that was defended by the old Lord De Clifford. It was thought to have been a great oversight in Somerset not to have occupied that garden-ground with his troops, since the enemy, by seizing it, placed the barrier, as it were, between two fires; the camp-field of York being on one hand, and Warwick on the other. Accordingly, when Warwick took possession of it, he gained the barrier almost by the same onset, and drove back the king's troops through the narrow lane of Sopewell into the inner part of the town, with dreadful slaughter. There it was that De Clifford, Somerset, and several other persons of rank fell. This ground of the battle is closely overlooked from the tower of the Abbey.

Why meet'st thou not the Ragged Staff?—p. 181.

The Bear and Ragged Staff, the well-known device of Richard Nevill, the great Earl of Warwick, called the King-maker.

Great Warwick's hardiness to prove.—p. 187.

This potent lover and promoter of turmoil lies interred in the choir of Tewkesbury Abbey. On

the roof of the fine monument, raised over him by
his Countess, is his image in armour. His beaver
is up; and his face has a spectre-look, that harmo-
nizes well with the gloom and the ancient story of
this venerable pile. The simplicity of the person,
who showed the church about twenty years since,
and the effect of these circumstances upon him,
were amusing. Pointing to the figure, he said a
stair led to the platform of the monument where it
was placed, and that "he had once been up at him,
and that he looked very ghastly." This was said,
with a sort of shudder, by a man nearly six feet
high, with a bald head, and of a grave aspect.

But Buckingham's pale plume he knew.—p. 193.

The Duke of Buckingham's vizor was pierced by
an arrow, but the wound was not mortal. He was
slain afterwards in the battle of Northampton, in
the year 1459, fighting for King Henry, near his
tent. His body was interred in the Church of the
Grey Friars in that town.

But, yonder, on St. Peter's way.—p. 194.

The slaughter was very great in this street, the
breadth of which permitted a more general contest;
and in which the Lancastrians made their last
stand. A great number of those, who fell there,

were buried in St. Peter's church-yard. Stowe says "it was stuffed full with their bodies."

Not thus she fled, when second war.—p. 196.

The battle of Bernard-heath, where Margaret of Anjou was victorious over the Yorkists.

And wounded, bleeding, fainting, slow.—p. 197.

Henry was slightly wounded in the neck by an arrow. He took refuge in a thatched cottage, a baker's, where he was discovered and surrounded by the Duke of York's party. The Duke, with several of the Yorkist chiefs, soon after visited him there, with much appearance of sorrow for what had passed and with a pretence, that the battle had been brought on by a misapprehension. They even besought pardon of Henry on their knees, and received it, with a stipulation, that they should immediately put an end to the slaughter. This done, the Duke conveyed the King to the Abbey, and placed him in sanctuary, close to the Shrine of St. Alban, whence he afterwards conducted him to the royal apartments of the monastery, there to remain in His custody, till the following day, when he should be conducted to London.

Lay Gloucester in his grave.—p. 208.

The stately tomb of Duke Humphrey forms the south side of the Saint's Chapel, now the Presbytery, behind the altar. There formerly stood the great shrine of the Martyr. The beautiful gallery, once used by the monks, who watched the shrine, nearly fills up the north side of the chapel; the east end was occupied by the shrine and by three tall, pointed arches, whose mouldings still ornament the wall, that supports the east window above. Athwart the western side stretches that lofty and beautifully carved screen, which separates it from the altar. On the pavement, near the spot where the shrine stood, is a trap-door, somewhat in the shape of a lozenge, which opens upon the vault under the monument of Duke Humphrey. The clerk, or sexton, unlocks and lifts this door; and, from the high windows above, the light of this world is let down at once, upon the open coffin and the bones of persecuted Gloucester. When you recover from the silent awe, into which this sudden spectacle of mortality has thrown you, you observe only a few large bones lying within the loose and .curled lead, in which the body was found, inclosed within a large oaken coffin. The vault is not deep, and the coffin lies close at the foot of the five narrow steps that descend into it; the light thus slanting in a strong line, falls upon the head of the coffin where the bones are placed. The skull is not there. After these awful reliques, the stately monument above strikes you forcibly, as a vain and melancholy pageant.

It was close to this tomb of his uncle and faithful friend, that Henry VI. himself a prisoner, took refuge after the battle, with the consent of his conqueror; a battle, which had probably never been fought, had Gloucester been alive to assist the councils of his nephew. What must have been the feelings of the venerable Abbot, while he stood beside the captive King and his Victor over the grave of the good Duke, once his fellow-student and patron, whose troubles he had foreseen and shared, and whose virtues he had honoured with the magnificence of a tomb worthy a crowned head. Gloucester had been a great benefactor to the Abbey. The manor of Pembroke in South Wales was among his bequests.

And from his memory threatened soon to sweep.—209.

Henry had already, from October 1453, to December in the following year, been afflicted with a total loss of memory. He had been recovered only about five months before the battle. A letter published by Mr. Fenn, in the first volume of his Collection, signed Edmund Clare and addressed to John Paston, mentions the King's illness and recovery, and conveys some interesting traits of his character from an account given by himself. His first act after his recovery was a command to his Almoner, to ride to Canterbury with his offering. When the Queen came to him, she brought the young Prince, his son, and he expressed much joy and thankfulness, that he had been baptized, and that he had been named Edward. Having asked who were the sponsors, " the Queen told him and he was well apaid (content.) And she told him that the Cardinal (John Kemp, Archbishop of Canterbury) was dead; and he said he knew never thereof till that time; and he said one of the wisest lords in this land was dead. And my lord of Winchester (William of Wainfleet, Bishop of Winchester) and my lord of St. John's (Robert Botill, Lord Prior of St. John's of Jerusalem) were with him on the morrow after Twelfth day, and he spake to them as well as ever he did; and when they came out they wept for joy. And he saith he is in charity with all the world, and so he would all the lords were."

The following extract from a letter in the same
Collections presents a curious picture of the times,
as well as of the anxiety of the Yorkists to conceal
their real designs and to recover the King's favour.

" And, Sir, as touching all manner of new
tidings, I know well ye are avarous (eagerly de-
sirous); truly the day of making this letter there
were none new, but such I heard of ye shall be
served withall.

" As for the first, the King, our Sovereign Lord
and all his true Lords stand in health of their
bodies, but not all at hearts-ease as we are.

" Amongst other marvel, two days afore the wri-
ting of this letter there was a language between my
Lords of Warwick and Cromwell, afore the King;
insomuch as my Lord Cromwell would have excus-
ed himself of all the stirring or moving of the male
journey (battle) of St. Alban's; of the which excuse
making my Lord Warwick had knowledge, and in
haste was with the King, and swore by his oath,
that the Lord Cromwell spoke not truth, but that
he was the beginner of all that journey at St.
Alban's; and so between my said two Lords of
Warwick and Cromwell there is at this day great
grudging, insomuch as my lord of Shrewsbury
hath lodged him at the Hospital of St. James (now
St. James's Palace) beside the Mews, by the Lord

Cromwell's desire, for his safeguard. And also all my Lord of Warwick's men, my Lord of York's men, and also my Lord of Salisbury's men, go with harness, and in harness, with strange weapons; and have stuffed their Lord's barges full of weapons daily unto Westminster.

" And the day of making of this letter there was a proclamation made in the chancery on the King's behalf; that no man should bear weapon nor wear harness defensible. Also the day before the making of this letter there passed a Bill both by the King, Lords, and Commons, putting Thorp, Joseph, and my Lord of Somerset in all the default; by the which bill all manner of actions that should grow to any person, or persons, for any offences at that journey done in any manner of wise, should be extinct and void, affirming all things done there, well done ; and nothing done there, never after this time to be spoken of; to the which bill many a man grudged full sore now it is passed.

" Written at London, on Saint Margaret's Even, in haste; and after this is read and understood, I pray you burn, or break (tear) it, for I am loth to write any thing of any lord; but I must needs, there is nothing else to write." The letter is signed " Henry Windsor."

Just cumbered with his crown of care.—p. 210.

Henry VI. was crowned by Archbishop Chichely, at Westminster, in the year 1429, being then not quite eight years old. In the great pressure of the crowd on that occasion, a priest and a woman were trampled to death.

And royal lodge, a stately pile.—p. 215.

The buildings called the Royal Lodging were separated from the rest of the monastery, by a range of cloisters running nearly the whole length of the church, but divided from it by the great square and by all the principal buildings of the convent. The Royal apartments were quietly and pleasantly situated near the southern edge of the hill, on which the town stands, overlooking the valley of the Ver.

Audience of him they still call King.—p. 216.

In pursuance of the policy, which masqued the views of Richard and which dictated the pretence of fighting *for* the King *against* his person and authority, the Yorkists asserted, that a letter had been despatched for the King, on the morning of the battle, and intercepted by Somerset, who never delivered it to Henry. But they never produced the bearer of this letter. It appears, however, from the letter of Henry Windsor, quoted in a former note, that a sincere dispute did exist between some of the chiefs of the party, as to their degrees of guilt in bringing on the battle; so that, if the proposal to compromise was never really made, there probably had been, at least, such a show of it as deceived many.

The Earl of Warwick was made Constable of Calais, either on the evening after the battle, or on the morning following; the Duke of York, Constable of England; Lord Bourchier, Treasurer of England.

It was but harness, thrown aside.—p. 222.

. " The Earl of Wiltshire, Thomas Thorpe, Lord Chief Baron of the Exchequer, and many others fled, and cast away their harness in ditches and woods." —Stowe.

There lay Earl Stafford, wounded sore.—p. 246.

Humphrey Stafford, Earl of Stafford, son and heir of the Duke of Buckingham, was wounded by an arrow in the hand. He was conveyed away from St. Alban's in a cart, as were several other wounded nobles. He died of this wound a few days afterwards.

Scarce word shall live, nor sign, to show.—p. 255.

Very few of the brasses remain, that adorned and identified the numerous grave-stones of abbots, monks and knights, who rest within the walls of this Abbey, in choir or chancel. The indented stone alone faintly shows the image, where the recording brass has once been. One of the largest brasses was torn off, within memory, because it had become unriveted at a corner, that turned up and caught the shoes of passengers ! There is not any memorial left at St. Alban's of Lord De Clifford, or of any of the other nobles, who fell in the first battle and who are elsewhere recorded to have been buried here, in the Lady Chapel, or in the Nave. See Weaver. The glaring white-wash, with which the most venerable walls of this church are disguised, has effaced every memorial inscription—four only excepted; one on Duke Humphrey; one on Sir John Mandeville, the traveller; a third on the Hermits entombed near the south wall; and a fourth recording that the Parliament, during the Plague of ......, sat within this Nave. The whitewash, seizing on what Cromwell's soldiers had suffered to escape, has spread oblivion over every thing, and has destroyed the finest effect of this ancient edifice, in the gloom, that once wrapt its vaults and pillared arches.

On bier and shield while soldiers bore.—p. 259.

The Infirmary of the Abbey, with the garden bearing its name, adjoined the south-west end of the church, communicating with the cloister, which opened to the south aisle by the beautifully-carved door, with a canopy of fretworked stone, which is still seen there.

Some were in 'bossed and damasked steel. p. 259.
And showed a casque of steel and gold.—p. 270.

Helmets were sometimes, at this period, stamped with a scroll pattern, resembling that formerly used for folding screens, and with which some chambers in Holland are still hung instead of tapestry. A helmet, which still retains a few traces of the damask pattern, stamped either on it, or on its leathern covering, is shown at St. Alban's, in St. Peter's Church. The leather, however, is entirely gone. It was dug within the walls of the ancient chancel, now pulled down, and was found near the spot where formerly the altar stood; a spot now part of the church-yard, which is slightly penned round, like a sheep-fold! It is painful to see a place once dedicated to sacred purposes, once the site of a Christian altar, preserved with so little reverence. It was many years since, but within the memory of some old persons still living (between the years 1802 and

1808) in the town, that this helmet was dug up. It had been probably interred with one of the victims of the first battle, great numbers of whom were buried at St. Peter's. That this helmet belonged to a person of some distinction is certain, from the situation, in which it was found—near the altar. The clerk, who showed it, could give no information, as to any epitaph, or circumstance, that might direct conjecture to the name of its late owner. Weaver, who mentions only such of the buried as had inscriptions remaining in his time, notices only three,—Sir Bertin Entwisel of Lancashire, and the elder and younger Bapthorp, whose fall is thus recorded:—

" Raph Bapthorpe, the father, and Raphe, the sonne, of Bapthorpe, in the East Riding of Yorkshire ; which, for many descents, hath yielded both name and reputation to that knightly familie ; fighting in this towne under the banner of King Henry the Sixth, lost their lives, and here lye buried together." Weaver then gives their epitaph, but does not say in what part of the church they were buried. The tomb of Sir Bertin, he tells us, was " under the plase of the Lectorium in the quyre, whereas a memorial of hym ther yet remeyneth."

As far, therefore, as we depend upon Weaver for instruction, we have no choice but to suppose, that this curious and interesting helmet belonged to one

of the former warriors. It is entire in all its parts
of head-piece, vizor, beaver, and chin, or neck-piece;
and that it is of proved iron was sufficiently, though
somewhat irreverently, shown by several hard blows
from the vestry poker, designed to move the beaver, which was held fast by rusted rivets. This beaver seemed never to have been intended to be raised
with the vizor, but could be lowered over the chin-
piece; from which it might, perhaps, be a little
lifted to unite with the vizor, when that was worn
down. On the edge of the helmet is the very place
where the plume, or crest, had been fastened. This
most curious relique showed no symptom of decay,
or weakness, from time; but, within, it exhibited a
very interesting proof that its owner had been in
more than one battle. On the right side of the head-
piece was the sign of a violent blow, from the full
effect of which it had saved its master for that time;
the helmet, it was plain, had been repaired after
sustaining this blow, for the patch and its rivets are
distinctly visible on the inside, though, without, there
is no appearance of either. It had been lined with
green cloth or baize, as some remains yet prove.
The vizor and beaver are of the same sturdy and
still tough iron as the head-piece and neck piece, on
which last the rivets, that once fastened it on to the
body-armour, are thickly set and entire. The old

persons, who remember this helmet in its earlier state, tell that it was covered with gilt leather, of which the stamped scroll lines seem to bear witness. With this casque were shown some large leg-bones, which were handled just as Shakspeare's gravedigger turns about the skulls;—merriment upon the passive bones of those, who have been !—merriment of that short superiority—that little " brief authority," some worse exercises of which " make the angels weep !"

Darkling, a watch-monk doth abide.—p. 322.

There is still in the wall an oven-like arch, holding a small bench, where one of the watch-monks sat, who guarded the shrine in the south transept.

Then onward, through the eastern arch.—p. 322.

This last arch, which opened upon a painted window, that once most beautifully terminated the long vista of the south aisle, is now bricked up; and all beyond, consisting of the ante-porch of the Lady Chapel and the chapel itself, is entirely excluded from the church. In this ante-porch were several dedicated altars and fine stained windows, whose fretwork is either filled up with bricks, that darken the place, or, being entirely deprived of glass, admits the swallows, whose nests are in the trefoil tracery.

The floor is unpaved, and obstructed by the inequa-
lities of the graves, the summits of which are heaped
upon it. You shudder as you pass over this dark un-
even floor and that of the ante-chapel, which sinks
so much towards the centre, that it seems as if you
were stepping among and almost touching the bones
of the numerous dead buried there. It was in this
porch and in the adjoining chapel, that the warriors,
killed in the first battle of St. Alban's, were mostly
buried ; not a single grave-stone now remains.

The chantry of St. Blaize pass by.—p. 322.

Bishop Blaize had been an early benefactor to
this Abbey. His chantry was in the ante-chapel of
the Lady Chapel.

Who, from the roof, shall on thee smile.—p. 323.

The portrait of Offa was painted on the roof of
the upper north aisle.

Where Michael and St. Patern bend.—p. 323.

An altar dedicated (according to the perversions
and superstitious modes of the Roman Cathol
ritual) to these saints, stood in the transept, bearing their images, which, on the days of their several
festivals, were carried in procession through the
town.

Of loftiest grace and beauty rare.—p. 324.

Three lofty, pointed arches, behind the Saint's chapel and shrine, and which once opened upon the porch and Lady-chapel, may still be traced upon the wall. They resemble the three fine arches in Salisbury Cathedral, in a similar situation, opening into St. Mary's Chapel. Before these of St. Alban's were filled up, the perspective from the western door of the nave must have been one of the grandest in England. The effect must have been heightened by the transverse lights, that fell from the distant windows of the Ante-chapel, and by the gradations of narrower and lower arches there, withdrawing beyond the tall ones of the shrine.

Eastward Fitzharding cast his eye.—p. 324.

At the south-east corner of St. Mary's Chapel is the Oratory, which was allotted by the Abbey for the observance of masses for the dead. It is now called the Vestry; but is closely locked up, during the ordinary days of the week, although, as appears, scarcely ever used, except on Sundays, when the boys of a Sunday school there receive some useful instruction.

Where St. Amphibalus long slept.—p. 331.

The reliques of St. Amphibalus were so rever

by the monks of St. Alban's, that, in the year 1178, they removed them hither from Redbourn, the burial-place of St. Amphibalus after his martyrdom. Abbot Thomas Delamere, in after-times, enriched his shrine, and decreed, that a Prior and three monks should be appointed to the care of his remains, with a yearly allowance of twenty pounds.

And wheaten sheafs and roses spread.—p. 339.

The altar-screen, at St. Alban's, though one of the finest in England, is not comparable to that at Winchester for richness and beauty of workmanship. The lightness of the latter gives it a resemblance to fine lace. Not a statue remains to occupy the highly ornamented large and small cells at St. Alban's. This screen was begun in some of the last years of Abbot Whethamstede, and finished during the time of Abbot Wallingford. Both abbots contributed largely towards it from their private fortunes. The arms of Whethamstede are carved over the left door of this fine screen.

Not then this beauteous screen appeared.—p. 340.

This very beautiful screen, which is said to have been brought to St. Cuthbert's chapel, once near the Abbot's cloister, is of the style of the fourteenth century, and in fine preservation. It was, perhaps,

of a more beautiful proportion originally, than the
great altar-screen, though less stately.   In few in-
stances can there be found a greater richness than
that of the spiry canopies of its fourteen largest
niches, or a better lightness than that of the double
open-work parapet, that runs along its summit.
Twenty smaller fretted tabernacles extend in a line,
below the large ones, now all alike deprived of their
images.   Two finely carved doors under pointed
arches open, on each side of the place where St.
Cuthbert's altar stood, into that part of the choir,
which is now called his Chapel.   The irregularity
of its design was probably occasioned by a necessity
for adapting it to a situation, for which it was not
originally intended.

And they to organs' solemn flow.—p. 350.

Abbot Whethamstede gave a " set of organs" to
the choir, which cost him above fifty pounds—a
large sum in those days.   At present, there is not
any organ in this venerable Abbey-church.   A
single oboe, played in the south transept, where it
leads the singing of the boys of the Sunday school,
is the only instrument, that now sounds within these
walls.   This simple oboe, however, swells sweetly,
and even solemnly, along the high roofs ; and sometimes a little robin, perched out of sight, is heard to

accompany it. The wild and solitary notes of this
little bird, breaking upon such a scene of ancient
story, where once the highest pomp of choral minstrelsy filled every vault and gallery with prayer
and praise from beings, whose bones now rest below,
awaken ideas; which cannot be described, but which
seem like recollections.

Of Richard's death in Pomfret tower.—vol. IV. p. 2.

In the sixteenth volume of the Archæologia, pp.
140, 141, 142, is a curious extract from a manuscript copy of Hardyng's Chronicle, preserved in
the Harleian Collection in the British Museum,
which copy contains the letter of Defiance, sent by
the indignant lords to Henry the Fourth, immediately before the battle of Shrewsbury.

Hardyng prefaces the letter by an explanation,
in which he says, " Truly I, the maker of this boke,
wase brought up fro twelve yere of age in sir
Henry Percy house to the bataill of Shrewsbury,
wher I wase with hym armed of xxv yere of age, as I
had been afore at Homyldon, Cokelawe, and at
divers rodes and feeldes with hym and knewe his
entent and hade it wretyn. Wherfore I have titled
in this booke that for trouth the cause why they
rose ayenst him may evermore be knowe."

Hardyng then says, that the cause was approved by

several persons of rank, who did not afterwards support it, " though they wer bounde to hym be theire lettres and sealls, which I saw and hade in kepynge whiles I wase with hym, and all theire quarell they sent to kynge Henry in the felde, writen under the sealless of their three Arms (the Earls of Northumberland and Worcester and Sir Henry Percy) be Thomas Knayton and Roger Salvayns quers of Sir Henry Percy; which quarell nowe followeth nexte after."

The Defiance (which is too long for this note) opens with an accusation, made in very solemn terms, against Henry Duke of Lancaster, that he, after swearing to them at Doncaster to claim nothing in the kingdom but his inheritance and that of his wife, had imprisoned his and their King in the Tower of London, until, under fear of death, he had renounced all his rights in England, France, and elsewhere; by colour of which resignation, he had crowned himself, he and his accomplices having collected, at Westminster, a crowd of the common people to salute him with their vociferations;—That, at the same place (Doncaster) and time, he had sworn, not to levy any tenths from the Clergy, or fifteenths from the people, or any other taxes, without the consent of the three estates of the kingdom in Parliament—notwithstanding which he had levied many taxes by his own authority;—That although he had also sworn, at the same place and time, that King Richard should reign and enjoy his full prerogatives, during his life, he (Henry) had imprisoned his sovereign in the castle of Pontefract, and caused him to perish by means horrid to relate —by hunger, thirst, and cold.

The letter contains some other charges; and there is a solemn eloquence in several parts of it, each head of charge commencing with—We declare and will prove; and each concluding with—Therefore are you perjured and false.

It must be admitted, however, that the letter proves against the writers themselves an intention of assisting, or, at least, of permitting Bolingbroke to obtain by force an influence over the exercise of the royal authority; for why, otherwise, should they receive his promise not to levy tenths, or other taxes, without the consent of the three estates? The quarrel seems to be another instance of a truth, which cannot be too often inculcated, that the contrivers of wrong generally become curses to each other, and have the evils they suffer aggravated by the consciousness, that they proceed from causes least apprehended by them—the ingratitude, or treachery of each other.

Who to his tomb the scar will bear.—p. 19.

Stowe (edit. 1592) says, "And at that battle were wounded lords of name. The King was shot in the neck with an arrowe: Humfrey Duke of Buckingham, and the Lord Sudley, in the visages with arrowes; Humfrey Earle of Stafforde, in the right hand, with an arrow; the Earle of Dorset was so sore hurt, that he might not go, but was faine to be caried home in a cart; and Sir John Wenlocke, knight, in like wise hurt, and caried from thence in a chair."

Certain rich robes, which once he wore.—p. 35.

On a subsequent occasion, when King Henry had passed his Easter at the Abbey, he gave, at his departure, his best robe, which he had worn only at this festival, and which his treasurer, knowing it to be the only one he had suitable for his appearance on high ceremonies, re-purchased for fifty marks, before he left the Abbey. This sum the King, however, directed to be laid out in gold cloth, of great value, called crimesyne thissue, and to be made up in one cope, a chasuble, and two tunics. It was, in fact, on this occasion, that he also begged of the Abbot and monks one favour,—" that they would appoint an anniversary to remember him

their benefactor; and that they would fix it by
the day of his death." This Obit was to be observed "for ever." Little did he conjecture, when
he made this affecting request, that the day from
which he would have it take effect, would be that
of his murder; and that the "for ever" of this
memorial would never commence, but the memory of him be forbidden, and his kingdom wrested
from his descendants. Even when it was won back
by a collateral branch of the Lancastrian line, it
does not appear, that this anniversary was ever remembered by his relative, though Henry the Seventh, by his will, appointed that an anniversary
should be observed for himself in this very Abbey;
for which purpose he left an annual stipend of "an
hundreth shelyngs." This will, besides showing the
contrast between the characters of the two sove-
reigns, affords throughout one of the most striking
and humiliating combinations of worldly vanity
and of a superstitious perversion of Religion, which
the weakness and inconsistency of the human mind
ever exhibited; and that too from a man of shrewd
perception and dextrous faculties, in temporary pur-
suits. Henry the Sixth, who would have been contented with a simple Obit, shows more good sense, on
many occasions, if you closely observe his conduct.

Henry the Seventh, not indeed in this place, but at
Westminster carefully stipulates for every circumstance of the ceremonies, that are to honour his
memory in the sepulchral palace, which he endows
with rich revenues, as if to console himself for the
loss of his earthly authority by a prospect of the
shadowy reign, the pageant power, that might exist
for him, after death should have put a seal upon his
worldly passions. Even the vestments, which he
bequeaths "to the Abbot, Prior, and Convent" of
Westminster, are to be thus ornamented—"the
whole suite of vestiments and coopes of clothe of
gold tissue, wrought with *our badgies of rede roses
and porteculleys,* the which we of late, at our proper
costs and charges, caused to be made and provided,
at Florence in Italie, that is to saie, the hoole vestiments for the priest, the deacon, and subdeacon,
and twenty-nine Coopes of the same clothe and
work." It is curious to observe how carefully the
white rose is excluded, and how duly the portcullis, the Lancastrian badge descending to him
from John of Gaunt, appears in every thing. Having directed that "an ymage of a King, representing
our owen person," shall be placed upon St. Edmund's shrine; he speaks of his crown as having been
obtained "with the victorie of our ennemey, at our

first felde." Then, with his usual minuteness, he
" adds, we woll that our said ymage be above the kne
of the hight of thre fote, soe that the hide and
half the breste of our said ymage may clierly
appere above and over the said Crowne; and that
upon booth sides of the said table be a conve-
nient brode border, and the same to be graven and
written with large letters, blake enamelled, these
words, Rex Henricus Septimus."—Will of K. Hen.
7th.

END OF NOTES ON ST. ALBAN'S ABBEY.

MISCELLANEOUS POEMS.

SALISBURY PLAINS.

STONEHENGE.

I.

WHOSE were the hands, that upheaved these stones
　Standing, like spectres, under the moon,
　Steadfast and solemn and strange and alone,
As raised by a Wizard—a king of bones!
And whose was the mind, that willed them reign,
　The wonder of ages, simply sublime?
　The purpose is lost in the midnight of time;
And shadowy guessings alone remain.

II.

Yet a tale is told of these vast plains,
Which thus the mysterious truth explains:
'Tis set forth in a secret legend old,
Whose leaves none living did e'er unfold.
Quaint is the measure, and hard to follow,
Yet sometimes it flies, like the circling swallow.

III.

Near unto the western strand,
Lies a tract of sullen land,
Spreading 'neath the setting light,
  Spreading, miles and miles around,
  Which for ages still has frowned :
Be the sun all wintry white,
  Or glowing in his summer ray,
Comes he with morning smile so bright,
  Or sinks in evening peace away,
Yet still that land shows no delight !

IV.

There no forest leaves are seen,
Yellow corn, nor meadow green,
Glancing casement, grey-mossed roof,
Rain and hail and tempest proof ;
Nor, peering o'er that dreary ground,
Is spied along the horizon's bound
The distant vane of village spire,
Nor far-off smoke from lone inn fire,
Where weary traveller might rest
With blazing hearth and brown ale blest,
Potent the long night to beguile,
  While loud without raves the bleak wind ;

No: his dark way he there must shivering find;
No signs of rest upon the wide waste smile.

V.

But the land lies in grievous sweep
Of hills not lofty, vales not deep,
Or endless plains where the traveller fears
No human voice shall reach his ears ;
Where faintest peal of unknown bells
Never along the lone gale swells ;
Till, folding his flock, some shepherd appear,
And Salisbury steeple it's crest uprear;
But that's o'er miles yet many to tell,
O'er many a hollow, many a swell ;
And that shepherd sees it, now here now there,
Like a Will o'-the wisp in the evening air,
As his way winds over each hill and dell,
Where once the ban of the Wizard fell !

VI.

Would you know why this country so desolate lies ?
Why no sound but the tempest's is heard, as it
      flies,
Or the croak of the raven, or bustard's cries ?
Why the corn does not spring nor a cottage rise ?

Why no village-Church is here to raise
The blest hymn of humble heart-felt praise,
Nor ring for the passing soul a knell,
Nor give to the dead a hallowed cell,
Nor in wedlock-bonds unite a pair,
Nor sound one merry peal through the air?
All this and much more would you know?   And
    why,
And how, Salisbury spire was built so high,
As fairies had meant it to prop the sky?
Then listen and watch, and you soon shall hear
What never till now hath met mortal ear!

VII.

It was far, far back in the dusky time,
Before Church-bells had learnt to chime,
That a Sorcerer ruled these gloomy lands
Far as old Ocean's southern sands.
He lived under oaks of a thousand years,
Where now not the root of an oak appears!
On each high bough a dark fiend dwelt,
Ready to go, when his name was spelt,
Down, down to the caves where the Earthquake
    slept,
Or up to the clouds, where the whirlwind swept.

VIII.

The Sorcerer never knew joy, or peace,
For still with his power did pride increase.
He could ride on a wolf from the North to South,
With a bridle of serpents held fast by the mouth;
And he minded no more the glare of his eyes,
That flashed about as the lightning flies,
Than the red darting tongue of the snake, that
      coil'd
Round his bridling hand, and for liberty toil'd.
He could sail on the clouds from East to West,
He rested not, he! nor let others rest;
And evil he wrought, wherever he went,
ᵃ For, he worked, with Hela's and Loke's consent.
ᵇ The BRANCH OF SPECTRES she gave for his wand,
And nine hundred imps were at his command!
He could call up a storm from the vast sea-wave,
And, when ships were wrecked, not a man would he
      save!
He could call a thunder-bolt down from a cloud,
And wrap a whole town in a fiery shroud!

   ᵃ ᵇ See the Notes at the conclusion of this Poem.

IX.

He could chase a ghost down the road of the dead,
  Through valleys of darkness, by snakes' eyes
      shown,
And pass o'er the bridge, that to Hela led,
  Where afar off was heard the wolf Fenris' groan,
While it guarded her halls of pain and grief,
  Where she nursed her children—Famine and Fear;
  He could follow a spectre, even here,
With the dauntless eye of a Wizard-chief.
He could chase a ghost down the road of the dead,
Till it passed the halls of Hela the dread.
He could chase a ghost down the road of the dead,
Till it came where the northern lights flash red.
Then the ghost would vanish amid their glow,
But the Wizard's bold steps could no farther go!
And whether those lights were weal, or woe,
The Sorcerer's self might never know.
All this and more he full often had done,
And changed to an ice-ball the flaming Sun!

X.

Now Odin had watched from his halls of light
This dark Wizard's fell and increasing might;

And clearly he knew, that his craft he drew
c From the Witch of Death and the Evil Sprite,d
Who, though chain'd in darkness, and far below,
Sent his shadows on earth, to work it woe.
This Wizard had even defied his power,
For once, in the dim and lonely hour,
When Odin had seen him riding the air,
And bid him with his bright glance forbear,
Great Odin's look he would not obey,
But went, on his cloud, his evil way!
He had dared to usurp, when invoking a storm,
The likeness of Odin's shadowy form,
And, when Odin sang his famed song of Peace,
That hushes and bids the wild winds cease,e
While it died the sleepy woods among,
And the moon-light vale had owned the song,
The Wizard called back the stormy gust,
O'er the spell-struck vale, and bade it burst!

c Hela.   d Loke.

e Odin boasts of possessing such a song. Had Milton seen
the boast of it in the Edda, when he wrote ?—

   " He, with his soft pipe and smooth-dittied song,
      Well knew to still the wild waves, when they roar,
      And hush the waving woods."

The woods their murmuring branches tossed,
And the song—the song of Peace—was lost—
Then Odin heard the groan of thrilling Fear
Ascend from all the region, far and near,
And, as it slowly gained upon the skies,
He heard the solemn call of Pity rise!

XI.

Then Odin swore,
By the hour that is no more!
By the twilight hour to come!
By the darkness of the tomb!
By the flying warrior's doom!
Then Odin swore,
By the storm-light's lurid glare!
By the shape, that watches there!
By the battle's deadly field!
ᶠ By his terrible sword and snow-white shield,
The Sorcerer's might to his might should yield.

XII.

While Odin spoke, the clouds were furled,
And those beneath, as stories say,

ᶠ The shield of Odin was said to be white as snow.

Lost the sight
Of our earthly light,
And caught a glimpse above the world!
But the phantasma did not stay :
It passed in the growing gloom away!
And from that hour these stories date
The fateful strife we now relate.

XIII.

Now, there was a Hermit, an ancient man,
Who oft lay deep in solemn trance,
Watching bright dreams of bliss advance ;
And marvellous things of him there ran ;
He had lived almost since the world began !
The people feared him, day and night,
And loved him, too, for they knew that he
Abhorred their wizard-enemy,
And wished and hoped to do them right.
HE OWNED THE SPELL OF MINSTRELSY !
And in the hour of deepest shade,
When he would seek his forest-glade,
(It was of grey oaks in a gloomy hollow
Where never footsteps dared to follow,)

And called from his harp a certain sound,
Pale shadows would stand in his presence 'round!
How this could be known, without a spell,
I must briefly own I never could tell.
—But, be that as it may—on that note's swell,
Whether they sleeping were in halls of light,
Or followed the stars down the deeps of night,
Or watched the wounded Warrior's mortal sigh,
Or after some ill-doing Sprite did fly,
On that note's swell they to the Hermit hie;
And heed his questions, wait on his command;
These were the Spirits white of Odin's band.

XIV.

Odin had marked this renowned old Seer,
   And to him, at times, his favour lent;
He was the first of the Druids here;
   And did all their laws and rites invent.
   Some stories say a Druid never bent
At Odin's shrine; and others may have told
The self-same tale, that here for truth I hold;
He was the first of all the Druid race:
   Owning the spell serene of Minstrelsy!

But though he oft the Runic rhyme did trace,
   No wizard he!
No fiend he called, no fiend he served,
And never had from justice swerved.
From mystic learning came his power,
His name was from his oaken-bower,
HE WAS THE FIRST OF ALL THE DRUID RACE!

XV.

And Odin had marked this renowned old Seer,
   And, when the solemn call for pity rose,
   This goodly man to do his bidding chose,
A sage like whom was found not far or near:
Upon his head the snows of ages lay,
   Hung o'er his glowing eyes and waving beard,
Touched every wrinkle with a paler grey,
   And made him marvelled at, and shunned, and
      feared;
   Yet, with this awe, love, as I said, appeared.

XVI.

He was gone to his home of oak;
   Starlight 'twas and midnight nigh;
Not one wistful word he spoke,
   But his magic harp strung high;

As he touched the calling string,
Hear it through the branches ring,
  Till on lower clouds it broke.
Straight in his bower dim shapes were seen
By the fitful light, that rose within,
And reddened the dark boughs above,
And chequered all the shadowy grove,
And tinged his robe and his beard of snow,
And waked in his eyes their early glow !
While, as alternate rose and sunk the gleam,
The tree itself a bower or cave would seem !

XVII.

The Druid, wrapt in silence, lay ;
  No need of words ; his thoughts were known ;
  " Odin has heard his people's groan,"
Spoke a loud voice and passed away.
Another rose, of milder tone !
" The mighty task is now thine own,
To free the land from wizard-guile ;
  If thou hast wisdom to obey,
And courage to fulfil the toil,
  Odin, for ages, to thy sway

Gives each long plain and every sloping dell,
Now suffering by the sinful Sorcerer's spell."

XVIII.

A third voice spoke, and thus it said—
  "Listen and watch ! for thou must brave
  The wily Wizard's inmost cave ;
And, while he sleeps, around his head
Bind a charm, that shall help thee draw
Each fang from his enormous jaw ;
There lies the force of all his spells.
Hundred and forty teeth are there
In triple rows ; his art they share.
Hundred and forty thou must draw,
From upper and from under jaw.
Quick must thou be ; for, if the charm
  Break, and his bond of sleep is o'er,
  Ere yet thy task is done, no power
Can save thee from his vengeful arm.
Thence from his cave, at magic's hour,
Speed thou ; and close beneath his bower
Bury the fangs nine fathom deep,
Or ere thine eyelids close in sleep :

With them his guile for ever laid,
Thine is the land, which late he swayed."

XIX.

The voice is passed, and once more stillness reigns:
The Druid's trance is o'er; yet he retains
    A wildered and a haggard look,
As pondering still the urgent word,
And wonderous call he just had heard.
    And sure instruction from that call he took!

XX.

And from this hour he was not seen,
    Neither on hill, nor yet in dale;
By the brown heath, nor forest green,
    Nor by the rills, where waters wail;
    By sun-light, nor by moonbeam pale.
But his shape was seen, by star-light sheen;
    Or so the carle dreamt, who thus told the tale!

XXI.

For many a night and many a day,
Close within his bower he lay,
For many a day and many a night,
Hid from sight, and hid from light,
Trying the force of his mystic might;

Working the charm should shield him from harm,
When he in the Wizard's cave should be,
  To set the wretched country free.
He owned the spell of Minstrelsy.

XXII.

It boots not that I here should say
What arts the Druid did essay :
  How with the misletoe he wrought,
    That twined upon his oldest oak,
  How midnight dew he careful caught
    From nightshade, nor the words he spoke,
When he mixed the charm with a moonbeam cold,
To form a web, that should fast enfold
The Sorcerer's eyes—vast Warwolf the bold.

  Nor boots it, that I here should say
The dangers and changes, that him befell
On his murky course to Warwolf's cell ;—
For, circled safe with many a subtle charm,
  Was his dark path along the forest-way ;
  The lamp he bore sent forth its little ray,
And sometimes showed around strange shapes of harm
Gliding beneath the trees, now close beside ;

G 2

Now distant they would stand, obscurely seen
Among the old oaks' deep-withdrawing green.

XXIII.

But the calm Druid touched th' according string
  Of the small harp he bore, with skill so true
    That straight they left their shape and faithless
        hue!
Then voices strange would in the tempest sing,
Calling along the wind, now loud, now low,
And now, far off, would into silence go:
Seeming the very fiends of wail and woe!
Again th' enchanting chord the Druid woke,
('Twas as the seraph Peace herself had spoke,)
And hushed to silence every wizard-foe.

XXIV.

  The story could unfold much more,
  That the daring wanderer bore,
  O'er valley and rock and starless wood,
  Ere at the Sorcerer's cave he stood.
There come, he paused; for even he, I ween,
Confessed the secret horrors of the scene.
A place like this in all the spreading bound

Of these low plains can nowhere now be found.
And scarcely will it be, I fear, believed
   That beetling cliffs did ever rear the head
   O'er lands as wavy now as ocean's bed.
But these huge rocks on rocks by might extinct were
      heaved.

XXV.

It was where the high trees withdrew their boughs,
   And let the midnight-moon behold the scene,
That hoary cliffs unlocked their marble jaws,
   And showed a melancholy cave between,
With deadly nightshade hung and aconite,
And every plant and shrub, that worketh spite ;
Upon their shuddering leaves the moonlight fell
But left no silver tinges there to tell
The winning power of simple Beauty's spell ;
   Nor touched the rocks, that hung in air,
   With glimpse of lustre, passing fair ;
A dull and dismal tinge it shed,
Such as might gleam on buried dead !
And led, as with a harbingering ray,
The Druid's steps, where the grim Wizard lay.

XXVI.

It led his steps ; but he, in silent thought,
  Stood long before th' expected cave ;
  For he beheld what none could brave,
Who had not yet with magic weapon fought ;
He stood, the unknown cave before ;
High shot the little flame he bore,
Then sunk as low, then spired again,
And gleamed throughout the Warwolf's den ;
It glanced on the harp at the Druid's breast ;
It brightened the folds of his gathered vest !
And chased the shade, that hung o'er his brow,
Bound with the sacred misletoe ;
It silvered the snow of his wavy beard,
  It showed the strong lines of age and care,
  But the lines of Virtue mingled there,
And wisdom benignant, yet stern, appeared.

XXVII.

Long before that cave he stood,
    For, hovering near,
    Dark shapes of fear
Among the nightshade seemed to brood,
And watchful eyes, between the leaves,

Now here, now there, portentous glare,
Direful to him, who fears and grieves,
   As meteors fly
   Through a troubled sky,
When the autumn thunder-storm is near.

XXVIII.

And thrice he turned him to the east,
  And sprinkled the juice of the misletoe;
And thrice he turned him to the east,
  And the flame he bore then changed it's glow.;
And thrice he turned him to the east,
  And the flame he bore burned high, burned low.
Then a solemn strain from his harp arose;
'Mong the leaves the watching eyes 'gan close;
One by one, they were closed in night,
Till sunk in sleep was the Wizard's might.
  For, by his art, the Druid knew,
    That Warwolf, though he lay unseen,
    His deepest, darkest cave within,
    Closed his eyes, when these eyes closed,
    And now in death-like swoon reposed.
And the Druid knew, that hitherto

The spell of Minstrelsy was true
But the Druid knew, that he must rue,
If the magic sound of his harping ceased
　Ere his terrible task was fully done ;
For Warwolf would wake, and, from spell released,
　Call from their slumber the fiends it had won.

XXIX.

The Druid knew this ; and he knew moreo'er,
　That, the moment he trod in the Wizard's den,
　Other fiends would spring from their sleep within,
　To clamour and curse, with a horrible din,
If he left not his harp at the cave's door ;
If he left it there, and the winds should deign
To call out it's sweet and magic strain,
The strain of his harp would with theirs contend ;
And if theirs were baffled, his toil would end ;
If their's should triumph, his life was o'er.
Yet he left his harp at the cavern door ;
But he traced a just circle where it hung,
And high in an oak's green branches swung.

XXX.

As now the Druid took his way
In the untried cave, where the Wizard lay,

Often he lingered and listened oft,
  Still the distant harp was swelling soft;
And he paced up the cave, without dismay,
Under scowling rocks, between shaggy walls,
Where the gleam of his lamp, as it faintly falls,
Shows a frowning face, or a beckoning hand,
Or a gliding foot, or the glance of a wand.
Yet oft at a distance he sweetly hears
The joy of his harp, and he nothing fears,
Till he comes, where a light now flashed and fled,
Which darted, he knew, from the Wizard's bed.
There opened the wall to a lofty hall,
And he viewed what must mortal heart appal. .

XXXI.

Outstretched and grim on his stony bed,
All ghastly-pale, like a giant dead,
With eyes half closed the Wizard lay,
His half-shut mouth his fangs display.
The skin of a dragon unscaled was his shroud;
  A rock was his bier; his watcher was Fear,
And the winds were his mourners shrill and loud,
  And the caverns groaned their echoes severe.

G 5

At his couch's foot lay a wolf at length,
But harmless in sleep was his sinewy strength,
'Twas the wolf he had ridden from north to south ;
All uncurled were the serpents, that bridled his
    mouth,
And the black, clotted stains might yet be seen
Of his yesterday's prey the teeth between.

XXXII.

The Druid approached, with caution and dread ;
The Wizard was pale ; but, was he dead ?
Here waited the Druid his harp's sweet sound.
It's note was now changed ; like a deep-drawn sigh,
He heard it's faint swell, and he heard it die ;
Then knew he full well, that danger was nigh.
He often and steadfastly looked around :
No spectre appeared in the dim-seen bound !
The Druid approached, with caution and dread ;
The Wizard was pale ; but, was he dead ?
As the Druid bent o'er that giant form,
    While his lamp glared pale on the haggard brow,
    And showed the huge teeth in a triple row,
He muttered the words, that will still a storm,
That can struggle with Loke and all his swarm.

XXXIII.

The mourning winds o'er vast Warwolf were still;
No breath from the Wizard's pale lips bodes ill,
Yet could not the Druid those fangs once view,
And know the task he was bidden to do,
Without feeling his very heart-blood chill.
He hung his lamp on a sharp rock near,
He bent again o'er vast Warwolf's bier,
And he touched one fang, with prudent fear.

XXXIV.

But, why does he start, and why does he stand
As though he saw Hela's shadowy hand?
He has heard the shriek of his harp afar!
He has felt the glance of his evil star!
And he hastens to fold his charmed band
Round the cold damp brows of his foe.
But not all the strength of his magic might
Can lift the head from its stony bed,
Or the strong bandage pass below,
To press the Wizard's forehead tight;
So he laid it loosely on the brow.

XXXV.

Then he took from the rock his faithful lamp,
And sprinkled the flame on the forehead damp.

Straight the head uprose, and the lips unclosed,
And each of the terrible fangs exposed.
And now he hastened to pass the band ;
He tied the knot with a shaking hand,
But tied it firm—he tied it fast,
That it might well and sure outlast
The struggle of every mighty pang.
And then he seized one hideous fang,
And threw it on the ground !
No blood escaped the wound.
Hark, to the harp's now rising sound !
He knew the fiends were fighting round it,
But he knew that his charmed circle bound it.

XXXVI.

And when he had seized the second tooth,
  He thought that he heard the Wizard sigh !
The third required the strength of youth,
  But he won it, and the Wizard unclosed an eye !
Senseless and dim, at first, it showed,
  But quickly a livid glare outspread,
  Which changed to a light of enraged red,
And strongly as a furnace glowed.

But the glow died away in the livid ray ;
And, touched by the spell, the eyelid fell,
Like a storm-cloud over the setting day.

XXXVII.

At the ninth drawn fang, the Wizard's hair
  Rose up and began to twine and twist,
Like serpents, and like to serpents hissed !
     Till it curled all on fire,
      In many a spire,
And the bridle-snakes, that lay on the ground,
Began to stir, and to coil them around;
And the wolf reared up his grisly head,
  And fiercely bristled his watchful ears ;
His foamy jaws grinned close and red,
  And a rolling fire in his eye appears,
As he looks back o'er the Wizard's bed.

XXXVIII.

Is that the harp ? or is it the wind,
Murmuring from the cave behind ?
It is the wind ! 'tis not the harp !
See ! Warwolf's face grows long and sharp ;
About his mouth a grim smile draws,
And the fiends know well his dire applause !

The charmed band can scarcely bear
　　The struggling of his writhing brow.
Watching that horrid strife, the Druid stood,
His harp's tones answered to his fearful mood;
Then he thought of the deeds of Balder good:
He muttered the Helper song of Odin;
He faced to the frost, that has fire within;
And thrice he bowed him o'er the bier,
　　Sprinkling the mystic misletoe.
Now Warwolf's fiendly smile is gone,
　　His brow is steadfast and severe;
　　Slow falls each hair to it's dark lair,
Quenched are the fire-snakes every one.
The wolf, half-raised on his worn claws,
Stands fixed as stone, with grinning jaws
And upward eyes, as watchful still
To do his Wizard's vengeful will;
His bridle of serpents, coïled o'er his head,
Remains, and their tongues are yet living-red;
But they dart no death, and no malice they shed;
And their hisses have ceased; for their venom is
　　　　dead!

XXXIX.

Hark ! hark ! afar what feeble note
Begins, like dawn of day, to float ?
Hark ! it is the rejoicing string,
  Sounding sweetly along the wind !
Never did mortal music fling
  Notes so cheering, notes so kind.
The Druid hoped, yet feared and sighed,
And then again his task he plied.

XL.

Three times nine of the fangs he drew,
And the Wizard did not change his hue !
Three times three and three times nine,
And his lamp more dimly 'gan to shine.
When he tried the very last fang of all,
  Warwolf lifted an arm on high ;
  And faintly waved the hand,
  That held the SPECTRE-WAND,
As though he would some evil Spirit call.
  His arm he did but feebly ply,
Like one, who, in an agitating dream,
  Mimicks some action of his waking hour,
Pursuing still his often-baffled aim,

And struggling with the wish, without the power,
To chase the phantoms, that all living seem!

XLI.

The SPECTRE-WAND had lurked within
The dragon's many-folded skin,
    That was the Wizard's shroud.
Now, firmly grasping that dread wand,
Which ne'er disowned its master's hand,
    He called on Hela loud!—
But he called Hela! once alone.
    Low sunk the muttered spell;
No fiends th'. imperfect summons own,
    His lifted arm down fell.
Now tried the Seer, but tried in vain,
The hateful SPECTRE-WAND to gain;
    Which still vast Warwolf's fingers grasped,
    As though his only hope they clasped,
Till every tendon seemed to strain.

XLII.

The Druid tried to break the wand,
    But, by its forceful charm secured,
And held, as if by iron hand,
    The mighty struggle it endured.

In the long strife the Druid turned,
   And spoke again dread Hela's name;
The Druid's lamp then faintly burned,
   Quivered again the failing flame.
He, by the signal undismayed,
   Another daring effort made:
   He tried again the last strong fang:
   The Wizard started at the pang,
But, though his lips moved at his will,
His wish they could not now fulfill.

   The wolf, though standing fixed as stone,
   Uttered one long and yelling groan;
·And his kindling eyes began to stream;
Then sunk the Druid's lamp's last gleam!

XLIII.

Oh! what is become of the harp's far sound?
   Sadder it mourns, and yet more weak;
   I hear it but faintly, faintly speak;
   And I see the Druid upon the ground
      In speechless alarm,
      Despairing his charm;—
The last of his spells had the fiends now found?

XLIV.

Whence is the light, that 'gins to wave?
  'Tis not his lamp, it's beams are shorn.
Nor fire, nor flame, through all the cave
  The Druid sees, aghast, forlorn.
But look not on the Wizard's bier,
For, the red light is streaming there,
  That threatens unknown ill;
Both, both his glaring eyes unclose!
The hall with lurid lightning glows;
  As if at Warwolf's will.
The harp, the harp! where is it's note?
I hear no distant music float!
     He tried to lift his head
     From off his rocky bed,
  But the charmed band was true and strong;
  Vast Warwolf's groans were loud and long,
And every mighty limb convulsive heaved.
  Could I have told the horrors of his face,
The tale, too fearful, would not be believed.
  Th' astonished Druid stood some little space;
So hideous and so ghastly was the sight,
That e'en his firmness viewed it with affright;

What then he thought may ne'er be told;
But what his fate this story may unfold.

XLV.

Then lifting his eyes from off the bier,
A pallid shade confronts him near.
It surely is the form of Fear!
It has her wild red look, her spectre-eye,
Her attitude, as in the act to fly;
Her backward glance, her face of livid hue,
Her quivering lip, dropping with coldest dew;
Her breathless pause, as waiting to descry
The nameless, shapeless, harm, that must be nigh!
He waved the BRANCH of SPECTRES o'er the bier;
'Twas Hela's self—the mother of wan Fear!
The Druid knew her by that dreadful wand
And by the glimpses of her flitting band.

When he saw the berried misletoe,
Profaned to conjure deeds of woe,
Fear was subdued, indignant ire arose,
The Druid-soul, disdainful of repose,
Knew not to tamper with his Order's foes.

XLVI.

She waved it o'er the half-gone Wizard's head ;
  A tremour crept upon his bloodless cheek ;
And see ! he turns upon his rocky bed,
  He moves his lips, that have not strength to speak.
She spoke : " Wake, Warwolf, from thy trance ;
  The phantoms of thy fate advance ;
Or wake not ; th' abject plain shall tell
The change, that still awaits thy spell.
The sun shall set, the moon shall rise ;
  Four and twenty hours shall go ;
The sun shall set, the moon shall rise ;
Then each oak of the forest dies !
  For thy bones shall have rule below."

XLVII.

With shaded eyes the Druid stood,
  Wrapt in dismay and fearful thought ;
But now, awaking from his mood,
  The last of all his spells he wrought.
Three bands he tore from his night-woven vest,
  And sprinkled the oil of his failing lamp.
The Wizard sunk on his bed in rest !
  Thrice on the ground did the Prophetess stamp,

And shook her streaming hair
In dæmon-like despair,
And stretched athwart the bier her withering hand,
And, shrieking, waved three times the Spectre-
Wand.

XLVIII.

At the first shriek, dark spreading mists appear;
And, in the midst, a Spectre, trembling Fear;
A wreath of aspin quivered round her hair.
More grisly pale than the Prophetess she;
More wild and haggard face could never be.
At the next shriek, distorted Pain,
With rolling eyes, that seemed to strain,
Started along th' affrighted ground,
With dreadful yell and fitful bound;
Even dark Hela shuddered, as he rose,
For Hela could not grant him short repose.
To the third shriek the Spectre-Branch waved
high.

A dim Shape came more dread than Pain or Fear;
Fell woe was in her eye, but not one tear!
A poniard in her breast, but not one sigh!

All ghastly was her face, and yet a smile
Was wandering on, but owned no thought, the
      while ;
Unnoticed blood distilled from her loose hair !
She spoke not, wept not, looked not—'twas Despair!

XLIX.

Hela, as touched by her cold hand,
  Stood, when she saw these shadows rise
To the false summons of her wand,
  Stood, like a wretch, who guilty dies.
" Ye come uncalled.   Why are ye here ?"
" We wait around vast Warwolf's bier."
" Ye come unwelcomed.   Hence, away !"
But Hela saw, with dire dismay,
Her children would no more obey.
They gathered round the Wizard's bed,
Despair drooped mutely o'er his head,
And Hela sunk, in mist, down to the dead !

L.

Then the flame of the Druid's lamp returned,
And as clear as the morning-light it burned,
    And the harp's triumphant sound
    Lightly danced the cavern round,

And filled the vaulted roof, on high,
With the loud song of truth and joy;
Through every hollow rock it rung;
   The Echoes tell not all the notes,
For ne'er before had they heard sung
   Such song as now around them floats.

LI.

At the first note, round Warwolf's bier,
The ghastly shadows disappear,
And a dark cloud began to rise,
That wrapt him from the Druid's eyes,
   Who gathered and counted the conquered fangs;
Then, thankful, from the cave he hies,
   To seek the lorn place, where the cymbal clangs
Of the Wizard's imp, as it watches his bower;
There to bury the teeth, at the magic hour.

LII.

From the mouth of the cave his harp he took,
   And hung it near his grateful heart;
The wires with answering rapture shook,
   And hope and courage did impart.
But its cautious master, true
To the whole task he had to do,

Bent, with tempered mind, his way,
Whither the Sorcerer's bower lay.
Through the forest he heard afar
　The cymbal's hoarsely-clanging jar,
Till he came to a widely-spreading plain,
Then ceased the Wizard's threatening strain;
　All was still as yon setting star.
But, for the bower he looked around in vain,
Unless that giant-tree be his strange bower,
A ruin now like him, and 'reft of power.

LIII.

In the centre it stood—a withered oak;
It's shadow was gone, and it's branches broke;
It's mighty trunk, knotted all round and round,
And gnarled roots, o'erspreading the ground,
Were proofs of summers that on it had shone,
And honours of old from the tempests won,
In generations all past and gone.
　And a scant foliage yet was seen,
　Wreathing it's hoary brows with green;
　Like to a crown of victory,
　On some old Warrior's forehead grey.

So reverend was it's look, it seemed to speak
    Of times long buried, that had passed it by
    And left it there thus desolate to sigh
To the wild winter-winds, in murmurs weak;
    A spectre of the woods, shadeless and pale,
    A form of vanished ages, whose dark tale
It once beheld, and seemed by fits to wail.

LIV.

Here came the Druid, with firm, silent tread,
To bury deep the fangs of Warwolf dread.
Now, by the waning Moon's red, slanting ray,
By her long, gloomy shadows on the way,
Two circles round about the oak he traced,
And, as with measured step and slow he paced,
And Runic words of secret import drew,
The mighty lines wider and wider grew,
As watery circles o'er a lake increase :
At length they rested, where he bade them cease.
Watching the minutes of the downward moon,
He walked th' enchanted Celtic circles duly o'er ;
    Dropping, at every bidden step, a fang.

One fang to every step he gave, no more,
  Meanwhile his harp, unsmote, with strange notes
    rang!
The vast circumference he paced not soon;
  One hundred and forty minute-steps past,
  Ere was paced the widest circle and last;
And the pale moon, behind the forest-shade,
  Sunk with a small and smaller curve of light;
O'er the wood-tops he watched her last glow fade,
  Till every lingering ray was lost in night.
The hour is won!—the spell is done!
The Druid to rest in his bower is gone!

LV.

Now LISTEN AND WATCH, and you shall see
What passed around that old oak-tree.
The marvellous story must now be told
Of the ban's last force of Warwolf bold.
When next the midnight-moon was seen,
The Druid returned to the forest green;
That forest green on yester-night,
Now mourned in all its leaves a blight!
And now were its branches shattered and bare;
Nor tree, nor bough, did the Sorcerer spare,

Dire was the hour when he waked from his swoon!
O'er all the region, far and nigh,
Far as the Druid cast his eye,
(Under the glimpses of the low-hung moon)
The lands all black and desolate lie!
But whither the Wizard his-self was fled,
And whether still living in trance, or dead,
Or what was become of his horrid den,
Were matters not reached by the Druid's ken.
Nor cliff, nor rock, was e'er seen from that hour,
On wilds, that had owned the Sorcerer's power;
Not an oak, or green bank, on hill or dale,
That once waved in Summer's and Winter's gale.

LVI.

The Druid pressed on through the lifeless wood,
Till he reached the plain, where the old oak stood.
Now listen and watch, and you shall see
What was done around that warrior tree.
Scarce could the Druid now believe,
That phantoms did not his eyes deceive,
As he looked o'er this desert land,
Far as his vision could command.

Is it the light, that mocks his sight?
Or shadows, that now the low moon throws?
What dark and mighty shapes are those,
    Standing like dæmons of the night?
Nearer and nearer the Seer now goes,
Taller and taller the figures arose!
Astonished he saw, on the plain around,
In the circles he traced on the teeth-sown ground,
A hundred and forty figures stand,
A lofty and motionless giant-band!
He paused in the midst, and calmly viewed
Their strange array and their sullen mood.
High wonder filled his mind, as this he saw.
And wonder still and reverential awe,
From age to age, have filled the gazer's mind,
With sweet yet melancholy dread combined.
Stonehenge is the name of the place this day,
But what more it means no man may say.

LVII.

Who, that beholds these solid masses rude,
Could guess they ever were with life endued?

And yet, receive the marvel that I tell,
These mighty masses held the Wizard's spell!
They were his buried fangs, and upward sprung
By nerve of magic, which they yet retained,
Dilating to enormous size and shape,
While from their prison-grave they strove t' escape.
But here their effort ceased, and, wildly flung,
They in their mighty shapes have since remained.
Their effort, but not yet their power, has ceased,
For, as the ages of the world increased,
Still with the charm of wonder they have bound
   Whoever stepped in their enchanted ring,
And when the learned held the truth was found,
     The daily and the nightly thought,
     So long pursued, so closely caught,
   Has proved a feather dropped from Fancy's wing!
And thus have two thousand ages rolled,
But the truth till now was never told!
     Unsuspected it lay,
     Closely hid from the day,
     Till some smatterer bold
Should the secrets of Druid lore unfold.

LVIII.

The Hermit, by the wondrous vision won,
  Felt not the shuddering earth, nor heard the gale
O'er the far wilderness come sweeping on,
  With gathering strength and wildly sweeping yell,
Till, like some fiendly voice it burst around,
And gradual died along the hollow ground.
    Then he knew it the Wizard's blast;
    It was his fiercest and his last,
And came for vengeance on the Druid's head;
But with his fangs his evil power was fled.
And, when rung out the harp's rejoicing swell,
The Druid knew that all was once more well.
Then to his bowery home his steps he turned,
And slept the sleep by conscious virtue earned.
His fortitude the Wizard's spell had braved;
His patient wisdom a wide land had saved!

LIX.

From forth that day began the Druid sway
  O'er all this widely stretching plain,
And hamlets few that on their border lay.
  Still did the Druids long remain

In the lone desert, far from vulgar eye,
'Wrapt in high thought and solemn mystery.
The circle of the Wizard's fangs, 'tis said,
  Was their great temple, where, on certain days,
In triumph for the tyrant-dæmon fled,
  They gathered from the country far around,
And sang, with nameless rites, their mystic lays,
  Here on this rescued memorable ground.

LX.

And thus they ruled, for age succeeding age.
  There is one later record, which doth spell,
But in what scroll, or rhyme, or numbered page,
  Or letter black, or white, I cannot tell—
There is one record, could it now be found,
Doth spell the words which, spoken on that ground,
  By the wan light of the setting moon,
  When night is far past her highest noon—
Words, that make sight so strong and fine,
As will the Druids' shadowy figures show,
When in their long and stately march they go,
  Around and round that mighty line,
Where yet the Wizard's fangs uprear
Their monstrous shapes upon the air.

And, as they glide those shapes between,
　　A beam-touched harp does sometimes shine,
Or golden fillet's glance is seen ;
While long devolving robes of snow,
Wave on the wind, and round their footsteps flow.
And then are heard the wild, fantastic strains,
Which Druid-charm has left to dignify these plains.

LXI.

Such was the scene, and such are the sounds,
Linked with the history of these grounds!
Nay, 'tis said that, at this very hour,
Without aid from any words of power,
If mortal has courage to go alone
To that remote circle and count each stone,
When the midnight-moon doth silently reign
Over the pathless and desolate plain,
Gliding forms may ev'n yet be viewed,
Of lofty port and solemn mood,
Performing rites ill understood
　　By people of this latter day !
　　How this may be I cannot say ;
For nobody of these days can be found
To venture alone to that distant ground,

j

When the midnight moon walks over the land,
With slow, soundless step and beckoning wand,
And cold shadows following her command.

LXII.

But, not for kindly sprites alone,
Is now that haunted region known,
Since the antique Seers are gone.
'Tis said that, sometimes, even there
Fiendish sprites will ride on the air!
To lone shepherd their forms appear.
Their forms in the tempest's first gloom he finds;
And this is the cause that the hurrying winds
Sweep so swiftly, and moan so loud,
As o'er those haunted downs they crowd.
On the waste's edge they gather and brood;
Then, meeting the wild fiend's fiercest mood,
They scud o'er the desert, through clouds, through
rain,
Like ship, with her storm-sail set, on the main.
While the Druids lived, these evil bands
Kept far aloof from the guarded lands.
But, when the last died, the Sorcerer's ban
Gained part of the force, with which it began.

LXIII.

And this is the cause why corn will not spring,
Nor a bird of summer will rest his wing,
Nor will the cottager here build his home,
Nor hospitable mansion spread its dome;
  Why the plain never hears merry peal,
  Announcing benefactor's weal,
  Nor e'en lone bell in village tower
  Knells the irrevocable hour;
Why the dead find not here a hallowed grave,
Why the bush will not bud, nor tall tree wave.
And why Salisbury steeple was built so high
As though fairies had reared it to prop the sky!
For the mischievous sprites they once came so nigh,
  They threatened all the country round,
  Castles and woods, and meadow-ground,
That kindly peer o'er the edge of the plain,
Like a sunny shore o'er a stormy main;
Nay, they came so near to Salisbury town,
The people within feared the walls would down.

LXIV.

Then they built a tower, as by charmed hands,
  So grand, yet so simple, its airy form!

To guard the good town from all fiendish bands,
   And avert the dreaded pitiless storm.
And they fenced the tower with pinnacles light,
   And they traced fine open-work all around :
It is, at this day, a beautiful sight !
And they piled on the tower a spire so high,
   That it looked o'er all the Sorcerer's ground,
And almost it vanished into the sky.
So lofty a steeple the world cannot show ;
   Nor, drawn on the air with the truth of a line,
   A form so majestic, so gracefully fine ;
Nor a tower more richly adorned below,
   Where fretted pinnacles attend,
   The spire's first ascent to defend,
And catch the bright purple of evening's glow,
While, sinking in shadows, the long roofs go.
     This spire, viewed by the dawn's blue light,
     Or rising darkly on the night,
As with tall black line to measure the sphere,
While stars beside it more glorious appear,
Has so holy a look, not of earth it seems,
But some vision unknown save in Fancy's dreams.

LXV.

Now this good spire thus high they made,
   All the land to watch and ward,
   That the ill sprites, whene'er they strayed,
To their confines might be awed.
It could see on the wide horizon's bound
Each shade, good or bad, as it walked its round,
      Whether a fairy or fiend,
      Whether a foe or a friend.
It could see the procession move along
   With glittering harps, in robes of white ;
It could hear the responsive far-borne song
Faintly swell o'er the wide-stretched plain,
Then sink, till all was still again,
   And sleeping in the clear moonlight.
So this beautiful spire did watch and wake,
And guarded the land for Innocence' sake.

LXVI.

   And, at this very day,
   Let but the feeblest ray,
Or gleam, of moonshine chance to fall
Over this steeple so slenderly tall,

Or but glimmer upon the trembling vane;
Though the 'nighted traveller on the plain,
While he perceives it faintly shine,
    Peering over upland downs afar,—
    Though he hails it for the morning-star,
Yet all too well the warning sign
Know the bands of the Wizard's line!
Soon as they spy its watching eye,
    Whether by moonlight, or by morn,
Sullen they sigh, and shrink and fly,
    Where sun, or moonbeam, never warn.
So this beautiful spire does watch and wake,
And still guards the land for Innocence' sake.

NOTES.

For he worked with Loke's and with Hela's consent.—
p. 113.

In the Edda, or system of Runic mythology, Loke was an evil sprite, or evil principle. The sixteenth fable of the Edda says of him: " As to his body, Loke is handsome and very well made, but his soul is evil, light, and inconstant. He surpasses all beings in that science, which is called cunning and perfidy.. Many a time hath he exposed the gods to very great perils, and hath often extricated them again by his artifices. His wife is called Siguna. He hath had by her *Nare*, and some other children. By the giantess *Angerbode*, or messenger of ill, he hath likewise had three children: one is the Wolf *Fenris*, the second is the great serpent of Midgard, and the third is *Hela*, or Death."

Of this Hela, the same fable says—" Her hall is
GRIEF; FAMINE is her table; HUNGER, her knife;
DELAY, her valet; SLACKNESS, her maid; PRECI-
PICE, her gate; FAINTNESS, her porch; SICKNESS
and PAIN, her bed; and her tent (or perhaps, her
curtains) CURSING and HOWLING. The one half of
her body is blue; the other half covered with skin,
and of the colour of human flesh. She hath a
dreadful, terrifying look, and by this alone it were
easy to know her."

The Branch of Spectres.—p. 113.

The miseltoe. The twenty-eighth fable, which
describes the death of Balder the Good, says, " that
the gods, together with Balder himself, once fell to
diverting themselves in their grand assembly; and
Balder stood as a mark, at which they threw, some
of them darts and some stones, while others struck
at him with a sword. But, whatever they could do,
none of them could hurt him; which was considered
as a great honour to Balder. At length, Loke, who
heard this, having possessed himself of the *mistiltein*
(the miseltoe), repaired to the assembly of the
Gods. There he found HODER standing apart by
himself, without partaking of the sport, because he
was blind. Loke came to him and asked him, why

he did not throw something at Balder, as well as the rest? ' Because I am blind,' replied the other, ' and have nothing to throw with.' ' Come then,' says Loke, ' do like the rest, show honour to Balder by tossing this little trifle at him; and I will direct your hand towards the place where he stands.' Then Hoder took the miseltoe, and Loke guiding his hand, he darted it at Balder; who, pierced through and through, fell down devoid of life; and surely never was seen, either among Gods or men, a crime more shocking and atrocious than this. Balder being dead, the Gods were all silent and spiritless; not daring to avenge his death, out of respect to the sacred place in which it happened."

In a note upon the subject of the miseltoe, M. Mallet says, " This plant, particularly such of it as grew upon the oak, hath been the object of veneration, not among the Gauls only (as has been often advanced without just grounds) but also among all the Celtic nations of Europe. The people of Holstein, and the neighbouring countries, call it at this day *marentaken*, or the ' Branch of Spectres ;'—doubtless on account of its magical virtues. In some places of Upper Germany, the people observe the same custom which is practised in many provinces of France:—young persons go, at the beginning of the year, and strike the doors and windows of

houses, crying, ' *Guthil*,' which signifies miseltoe.
(See Keysler, Antiq. Sept. p. 304. and *seq*.) Ideas
of the same kind prevailed among the ancient in-
habitants of Italy. Apuleius hath preserved some
verses of the ancient poet Lælius, in which miseltoe is mentioned as one of the ingredients which
will convert a man into a magician. (Apul. Apolog.
Prior.)" Mallet's Northern Antiquities, vol. ii.
p. 139. 143.

SHAKSPEARE'S CLIFF.

HERE, all along the high sea-cliff,
  Oh, how sweet it is to go!
When Summer lures the light-winged skiff
  Over the calm expanse below,—

And tints, with shades of sleepy blue,
  Misty ocean's curving shores;
And with a bright and gleaming hue,
  Dover's high embattled towers.

How sweet to watch the blue haze steal
  Over the whiteness of yon sail;
O'er yon fair cliffs, and now conceal
  Boulogne's walls and turrets pale!

Oh ! go not near that dizzy brink,
  Where the mossed hawthorn hangs its root,
To look how low the sharp crags sink,
  Before the tide they overshoot.

Nor listen for their hollow sound—
  Thou canst not hear the surges mourn,
Nor see how high the billows bound
  Among the caves their rage has worn.

Yet, yet forbear ! thou canst not spring,
  Like fay, from off this summit high,
And perch upon the out-stretched wing
  Of the sea-mew passing by,

And safely with her skirt the clouds ;
  Or, sweeping downward to the tide,
Frolic amid the seaman's shrouds,
  Or on a bounding billow ride.

Ah ! no ; all this I cannot do ;
  Yet I will dare the mountain's height,

Seas and shores and skies to view,
  And cease but with the dim day-light.

For fearful-sweet it is to stand
  On some tall point 'tween earth and heaven,
And view, far round, the two worlds blend,
  And the vast deep by wild winds riven.

And fearful-sweet it is to peep
  Upon the yellow strands below,
When on their oars the fishers sleep,
  And calmer seas their limits know.

And bending o'er this jutting ridge,
  To look adown the steep rock's sides,
From crag to crag, from ledge to ledge,
  Down which the samphire-gatherer glides.

Perhaps the blue-bell nods its head,
  Or poppy trembles o'er the brink,
Or there the wild-briar roses shed
  Their tender leaves of fading pink.

Oh fearful-sweet it is, through air
  To watch their scattered leaves descend,
Or mark some pensile sea-weed dare
  Over the perilous top to bend,

And, joyous in its liberty,
  Wave all its playful tresses wide,
Mocking the death, that waits for me,
  If I but step one foot aside.

Yet I can hear the solemn surge
  Sounding long murmurs on the coast ;
And the hoarse waves each other urge,
  And voices mingling now, then lost.

The children of the cliffs I hear,
  Free as the waves, as daring too ;
They climb the rocky ledges there,
  To pluck sea-flowers of humble hue.

Their calling voices seem to chime ;
  Their choral laughs rise far beneath ;

While, who the dizziest point can climb,
    Throws gaily down the gathered wreath.

I see their little upward hands,
    Outspread to catch the falling flowers,
While, watching these, the little bands
    Sing welcomes to the painted showers.

And others scramble up the rocks,
    To share the pride of him, who, throned
On jutting crag, at danger mocks,
    King of the cliffs and regions round.

Clinging with hands and feet and knee,
    How few that envied height attain !
Not half-way up those urchins, see,
    Yet ply their perilous toil in vain.

Fearless their hero sports in air,
    A rival almost of the crows,
And weaves fresh-gathered blossoms there,
    To bind upon his victor-brows.

The broad sea-myrtle glossy bright,
  Mixed with the poppy's scarlet bell,
And wall-flowers, dipt in golden light,
  Twine in his sea-cliff coronal.

The breeze has stolen his pageant-crown;
  He leans to mark how low it falls;
Oh, bend not thou! lest, headlong down,
  Thou paint'st with death these fair sea-walls!

Now, o'er the sky's concave I glance,
  Now o'er the azure deep below,
Now on the long-drawn shores of France,
  And now on England's coast I go,

To where old Beachy's beaked head,
  High peering in the utmost West,
Bids the observant seaman dread,
  Lest he approach his guarded rest.

What fairy hand hangs loose that sail
  In graceful fold of sunny light?

Beneath what tiny figures move,
  Traced darkly on the wave's blue light?

It is the patient fisher's sloop,
  Watching upon the azure calm ;
They are his wet sea-boys, that stoop,
  And haul the net with bending arm.

But on this southern coast is seen,
  From Purbeck hills to Dover piers,
No foam-tipt wave so clearly green,
  No rock so dark as Hastings rears.

How grand is that indented bay,
  That sweeps to Romney's sea-beat wall,
Whose marshes slowly stretch away,
  And slope into some green hill small.

Now North and East I bend my sight
  To where the flats of Flanders spread ;
And now where Calais cliffs are bright,
  Made brighter by the sunset red.

Shows not this towering point so high
  To him, who in mid-channel sails;
For the slant light from western sky
  Ne'er on its awful front prevails.

But mark! on *this* cliff Shakspeare stood,
  And waved around him Prosper's wand,
When straight from forth the mighty flood
  The Tempest " rose, at his command!"

THE FISHERS.

STEEPHILL.

BEHOLD this rocky bay! On either hand
Cliffs dark and frantic rise and stretch away
To yon bold promontories, East and West,
Hanging amid the clouds ; that shut out all,
Save seas and skies and sails dim-moving on
Th' horizon's edge, and the rough boat, that skirts,
With slow and wary course, this ruinous strand.
Far 'mong the waves, are shown gigantic limbs
Of these stern shores, whose out-post Terror is,
Whose eyes look down on desolation, pain,
Shipwreck and death.   Yet, half way up the rocks,
And scarce beyond the salt spray's reach, when
     storms
Of winter beat, perched where the sea-mew rests

In sun-beam, a low fisher's cabin peeps
From its green sheltering nook.   Wild mountainous
    shrubs
Hang beetling o'er it, and such flowers as grow
On rocky ledges, brought by the unseen
Air, messengers from off some fertile hill
Or dale, or haply from far forest's side ;
The scarlet poppy and the blue corn-flower,
The wild rose and the purple bells, that chime
In th' evening breeze to the poor woodlark's notes.
Full to the South, the fisher's cottage peeps,
And overlooks how many lonely leagues
Of ocean, sleeping in its summer haze
Of downy blue, or green, or purple, shades,
Charming the heart to musing and sweet peace !
How solemn, when our autumn's moon goes down,
And walks in silence on the farthest waves,
(Then sinks, leaving brief radiance in the air,)
To measure out a few short moments here,
By the sad, dying glow !

But sweet, O then, most sweet ! when the clear
    dawn

Of June breaks on, and blesses the horizon.
In holy stillness it dispels the shades
Of night, appearing like the work sublime
Of Goodness,—a meek emblem of the JUST
And LIVING GOD! Bending our heads with awe
And grateful adoration, we exclaim—
" FATHER OF LIGHT! Thou art *our* Father too ;
We are Thy creatures; and these glorious beams
Attest, that in THY GOODNESS we are made
For bliss eternal."

There stands the fisher's hut, and close beside,
A mountain-stream winds round the mossed plat-
        form,
Singing wild lullaby to the wailing surge,
As 'mid resisting brakes and massy crags,
It seeks a passage to the shore below.
There, hauled above the reach of flowing tides
And the high-bounding spray, the sea-boat rests,
Huge, sturdy, heavy, almost round, and formed
For labour and hard strife with the rough sea ;
About the fisher's cot, from crag to crag,

His nets hang round in many a graceful sweep,
'Midst his long lines and treacherous baits and hooks.
Beside his door, the aged fisher weaves
New meshes for his sons, and sends, at times,
A look far o'er the ocean, where the beam
O' the west falls brightest, for the adventurers,
Who yester-morn went forth, and all night long
Watched patient on the waters, and all day
Have hauled the net, or laboured at the oar.
More fearful roves his eye, as sinks the sun,
While sad he marks September's stormy cloud
Fire all the West, and tip with crimson hues,
Though less resplendent, ev'n the nearer waves
While the broad flush tinges his silver locks
And his brown visage and his garments blue.
Anxious, he throws aside th' unfinished web,
And climbs the higher crag, and thence afar,
Turning the western cape, he sees the glance
Of oars withdrawing, and the square sail set
And swelling to the breeze. With struggling toil
The poor bark seeks its home, ere night and tempest
Meet on the billows. While she thus, scarce known,

Alternate rides the ridge and then is lost
Below the shelving wave, widely they steer
Athwart the dangerous surge, though not that way
Lies their dear home ; but well they know where lurk
The rocks unseen, and where the currents flow.
Suddenly drops the sail, and now again
This way they bend, while, as they ply once more
The oars, just heard, and turn, with scrupulous eyes,
To view their narrow course, a faint ray shows
Their sun-burnt features and their ragged locks,
Beneath the sea-worn hat.   Nearer now they move,
And now scarce lift the oar, so cautiously
They creep along the strand, and wind their way
Among its half-seen rocks.

Stays the old fisher on the high crag now ?
No ; yonder down the steep path slow he steps,
And his wave-faring children hails afar.
Meanwhile upon the beach, patient and cold,
Stands the poor horse, with drooping head and eyes
Half-shut, and panniers all too wide and deep,
Waiting the cargo, that his master, tired

And sauntering on the water's edge, shall bring:
Then must he bear it up high cliffs and hills,
To the far vale, where lies some peopled town.
Now slowly grounds the skiff, and the glad fishers,
Mounting the beach, the bended grapple cast.
"What luck? what luck? my boys!"   "Good luck,
      my father!"
And forth they pour the treasure of the main,
With many a scaly form unshapely, strange!
The dog-fish monstrous, with his high, round back,
And look voracious.   Oh! ill-named is he,
After man's careful, tender, faithful friend!
The spotted Seston,* dragon-like, with wings
And jaws terrific; and the giant skate.
Then dark-mailed forms,† that die in torture wild,
Unfitted, therefore, for the feast of man,
To whom abundant *guiltless* food is given.
And last, a shape, the fairy of the wave,
Clad in transparent tints of silver comes.‡

---

* So called by the fishermen.   † Lobsters.
‡ Whitings.

But see where the last gleam of the day's sun,
Far from behind that western promontory,
Slants 'thwart the deep curve of this shaded bay,
Tinges yon headland of the eastern shore,
And goes in stillness down on the fair waves,
Seeming to say, " Children of Time, farewell !
Your course draws nearer to Eternity;
Even thus must fade your glory in this world :—
But sure as dark shades of the night lead on
To morning, the sun-set of earthly life
Leads to the dawn of an eternal day :—
Think of THAT DAWN !"

Now doth the aged fisher mutely watch,
While his stout sons fling o'er their shoulders broad
Deep osier baskets hung with pebbles round ;
Then, wrapt in his blue mantle, stalks away,
Beneath the dark cliffs beetling o'er the sea,
To those low rocks, that stretch, point after point,
Far out amid the tide, crowned with black moss.
There, in the waves, safe from rapacious force,
And from the eye of plunderer close concealed,
He leaves his treasure, for to-morrow's care ;

Then hies he homeward.   There, amidst the friends
He loves, reposes.   All last night, he watched
Upon the rocking main ; the arching sky
His sole, cold roof ; the stars his only guides
Through the vast shadow of the lonely deep !
This night, how calm his dream, how sweet his
          sleep,
In the safe shelter of his cabin small,
With his glad family round him hush'd in peace !

IN THE NEW FOREST.

WANDERER! if thy path bend o'er these lawns
And forest-lands, stay thy rejoicing steps—
Though they would fain bound with yon fawns and
    hinds
Down the green slope, and skim the level turf
To other slopes, and other pluming groves,—
Stay thy intemperate spirit, and mark well
Each beauty of the scene, and the strong lights
And stormy sunshine, that fall o'er these shades!
Pause thou awhile, that, in some future hour,
When the long sunless storm of winter broods,
And thou sitt'st lonely by thy evening hearth,
In melancholy twilight, listening
The far-off tempest,—then sweet Memory
May come, and with her mirror cheer thy mind,

On whose bright surface lovelier scenes shall live
Than any shrined within Italian climes;
And every graceful form and shaded hue,
As now it lives, again shall smile before thee :
For England, beauteous England, scarce can boast,
Through her green vales and plains and wavy hills,
Another landscape of such sylvan grace.

'Twas surely here, that Shakspeare dreamt of fays,
And in these shades Titania held her court,
And bade her tiny bands in starlight revel.
Those tufts of oak, that crown the swelling lawn,
Those were her shady halls at high moon-tide;
And yon light ash her summer-night pavilion,
Lighted by dew-drops and the flickering blaze,
That glances from the high electric north.
Where'er the groves retire and meadows rise,
There were her carpets spread, of various tints
From turf and amorous lichen, all combined
With soft flowers and transparent azure-bells,
On whose pure skin their purple veins appear.
And over all these hues a veil is thrown
Of silvery dew, oft lighted by the moon.

Temper thy joyous spirit, wanderer!
And 'gainst the wintry hour, when thorns alone
Hold forth their berries, cull sweet summer-buds.
Then shall the deep gloom vanish, the storm sink!
The balmy air of woods shall soothe thy sense,
And their broad leaves thy landscape canopy,
E'en in December's melancholy day!

And now bound with those fawns down the green
    slope,
Skim the smooth turf to other hills and groves,
In the full joy of sunshine and new hopes.

ON A FIRST VIEW OF THE GROUP

CALLED THE

SEVEN MOUNTAINS;

IN THE APPROACH TO COLOGNE FROM XANTEN.

———

WHEN first I saw ye, Mountains, the broad sun
In cloudy grandeur sunk, and showed, far off,
A solemn vision of imperfect shapes
Crowding the southward sky and stalking on
And pointing us "the way that we should go."
Dark thunder-mists dwelt on ye; and your forms,
Obscurely towering, stood before the eye,
Like some strange thing portentous and unknown.
I watched the coming storm. The sulphurous gloom
Clung sullenly round me, and a dull tinge
Began to redden through these mournful shades.
A low imperfect murmur o'er ye rolled.

Doubtful, I listened.   On the breathless calm
Again I heard it—then, ye Mountains vast,
Amid the tenfold darkness ye withdrew,
And vanished quite, save that your high tops
    smoked,
And from your clouds the arrowy lightnings burst,
While peals resistless shook the trembling world !—

A SECOND VIEW OF

THE SEVEN MOUNTAINS.

—

MOUNTAINS! when next I saw ye it was Noon,
  And Summer o'er your distant steeps had flung
  Her veil of misty light: your rock-woods hung
Just green and budding, though in pride of June,

And pale your many-spiring tops appeared,
  While, here and there, soft tints of silver grey
  Marked where some jutting cliff received the ray;
Or long-lived precipice its brow upreared.

Beyond your tapering pinnacles, a show
  Of other giant-forms more dimly frowned,
  Hinting the wonders of that unknown ground,
And of deep wizard-vales, unseen below.

Thus, o'er the long and level plains ye rose
 Abrupt and awful, when my raptured eye
 Beheld ye.   Mute I gazed! 'Twas then a sigh
Alone could speak the soul's most full repose ;

For of a grander world ye seemed the dawn,
 Rising beyond where Time's tired wing can go,
As, bending o'er the green Rhine's liquid lawn,
 Ye watched the ages of the world below.

ON ASCENDING A HILL CROWNED WITH

A CONVENT.

NEAR BONN.

———

Up the mossed steeps of this round hill we climbed,
  Tracking amid close woods our doubtful way;
When, high above, the lonely vesper chimed
  On the still hour of the declining day.
We paused to listen, and to taste awhile
  The pure air scented with the bruised herb;
And catch the distant landscape's parting smile,
  Ere the light breeze the shadowy boughs disturbed.
" Oh verdant foliage! in your dancing play,
  Hide not those soft blue lines, that northward
      swell,
  And of far mountain-regions faintly tell!
Wrap not in your high shades those turrets grey,

That rear themselves above the Rhine's broad flood,
  Where the slow bark, with wide, out-stretched
     wings,
  Her lengthening shadow o'er the waters flings."
Onward we pass amid the closing wood,
Till, once again emerging from the night,
  O'er a near ridge of darkest pine we spy
  The peaks of eastward mountains, peering high ;
Touched with gay colours and with sunshine bright,
  They draw clear lines on the transparent sky,
And lift their many-tinctured forms of light !

With weary step a convent's porch we found.
What music met us on that holy ground,
  Swelling the song of peace and praise to HIM,
Who clad with glory all the prospect round !
  Our full hearts echoed back the grateful hymn.
A turret's utmost height at length we gain,
  And stand as on a point above the world,
  Viewing the heaven's vast canopy unfurled,
  And the great circle's widely-spreading line
  Sink low, and softly into light decline.

There, in far distance, on the western plain,
　　Thy spires, Cologne, gleamed to the setting ray :
　　Thy useless ramparts and thy turrets grey
　　Hinted where still the cowled city lay.
Oh melancholy walls ! unlike the view,
That the sweet poet of Vauclusa drew,
When, wreathed with flowers, thy maidens fair advance,
　　vance,
With choral songs and steps of airy dance,
And to the Rhine's fleet wave,* on summer's eve,
Their blooming garlands and their sorrows give.

　　* Petrarch notices this ceremony in one of his letters. " The sun was declining : and scarcely was I alighted, when these unknown friends brought me to the bank of the Rhine, to amuse me with a spectacle which is exhibited every year, on the same day, and on the same place. They conducted me to a little hill, from whence I could discover all that passed along the river. An innumerable company of women covered its banks : their air, their faces, their dress struck me.................In the midst of the vast crowd this sight had drawn together, I was surprised to find neither tumult nor confusion ; a great joy appeared without licentiousness. How pleasant was it to behold these women ; their heads crowned with flowers, their sleeves tucked up above their elbows, with a sprightly air advancing to wash their hands and arms in the river. They pronounced something in their language, which appeared pleasing, but I did not understand

How changed the scene ! Now paler forms appear,
Wrapt in black garments and with brow severe;
And, as with shaded eyes they stalk along,
Receive poor homage from the passing throng.
Oh melancholy walls ! always, as now,
Be seen at distance on the landscape's brow !

That stretching landscape various shades o'erspread,
  Of yellow corn and bowery vineyards green ;
There the brown orchard reared its tufted head,
  And there the Rhine's long-winding light was
     seen,
With castles crowned was its rocky shore,
And famed for dismal tales in early lore.
Northward, the far Westphalian lands withdrew,
Line above line, in level tints of blue ;
While to the West, where forest hills extend,

it. Happily, I found an interpreter at hand ; I desired one
who came with me to explain to me this ceremony. He told
me it was an ancient opinion spread among the people, and
particularly the women, that this lustration was necessary to
remove all the calamities with which human beings are threatened in the course of the year ; and, when this was done,
they had nothing to fear till the following year, at which
time the ceremony must be renewed."

The long perspective lifts a pomp of shade,
Mellowed with evening lights, where sweetly blend
  Convents and spires, as if for peace-marks made.
Such were the scenes, that from the falling sun,
(When he his bright and blessed course had run)
Threw their long shadows, mourners of past day,
And then in stillness slept beneath his ray.
But other scenes a holier homage paid,
Where, eastward, pointing up the heavenly way,
Above the thunder's cloud and cloud of Time,
Those everlasting mountains stand sublime,
And to the sun's CREATOR lift the head !
Steadfast upon the Rhine's tumultuous shore,
Ye listened, Mountains, to the distant roar,
The battle-shout of nations now no more.
Ye viewed the suns of centuries go down,
  And smiled, as now, beneath their farewell beam ;
 . Ye saw the thunder-storms of ages gleam,
The elemental and the human frown,
And heard afar the mingled strife pass by
Into the silence of Eternity !
Unchanged amid the ever-changing scene,
  As in the world's first dawn, ye still appear,

With beauty bright, majestic, young, serene,
  Clothed in the colours of the various year.
While rainbow-colours indistinctly lay
On the lone summits, till, in slow decay,
They seemed like far-hung clouds on Evening's pall,
  Just purpled with a melancholy ray ;
While dark we saw the mountain-shadows fall,
  And steal the·valleys and the woods away !
Then all in paleness came the twilight-star,
  And, pensive, seemed to bend upon the West ;
As though she watched th' expiring sun afar,
  And bade, with tearful smile, his spirit rest !
Oh ! then how sweetly and how solemn rose
  The requiem-strains, that, in the parting hour,
  Beneath the sacred roof responses pour ;
While all without was hushed in deep repose.
The air's soft breathings scarce were heard to die,
  Save when among the braided vines it crept,
And waked the quivering tendril with its sigh.
  Thus earth and air their hour of slumber kept !
  All but the stars ! Slumbering too long in light,
They now through shade their opening eyes reveal,
  In trembling glances, to their empress—Night,
Keeping high watch till forth the Morning steal,

From adverse darkness.   Self-supported, great,
Ye, tranquil 'mid the louring storms of fate,
Rise, like the honest mind, in the dread hour,
When stern Adversity tries Virtue's power :—
Thus ye, distinguished through the fearful gloom,
A steadfast strength and brighter mien assume.
Thus, 'mid the changing lights, that life pervade,
    May we, like you, assailing clouds dispel—
Grateful in sunshine—steadfast in the shade !
    Farewell ! ye awful monitors, farewell !

THE SNOW-FIEND.

———

HARK! to the Snow-Fiend's voice afar
That shrieks upon the troubled air!
Him by that shrilly call I know—
Though yet unseen, unfelt below—
And by the mist of livid grey,
That steals upon his onward way.
He from the ice-peaks of the North
In sounding majesty comes forth;
Dark amidst the wondrous light,
That streams o'er all the northern night.
A wan rime through the airy waste
Marks where unseen his car has past;
And veils the spectre-shapes, his train,
That wait upon his vengeful reign.

Disease and Want and shuddering Fear
Danger and Woe and Death are there.
Around his head for ever raves
A whirlwind cold of misty waves.
But oft, the parting surge between,
His visage, keen and white, is seen;
His savage eye and paly glare
Beneath a helm of ice appear;
A snowy plume waves o'er the crest,
And wings of snow his form invest.
Aloft he bears a frozen wand;
The ice-bolt trembles in his hand;
And ever, when on sea he rides,
An iceberg for his throne provides.
As, fierce, he drives his distant way,
Agents remote his call obey,
From half-known Greenland's snow-piled shore
To Newfoundland and Labrador;
O'er solid seas, where nought is scanned
To mark a difference from land,
And sound itself does but explain
The desolation of his reign;

The moaning querulous and deep,
And the wild howl's infuriate sweep
Where'er he moves, some note of woe
Proclaims the presence of the foe;
While he, relentless, round him flings
The white shower from his flaky wings.
Hark! 'tis his voice:—I shun his call,
And shuddering seek the blazing hall.
O! speak of mirth; O! raise the song!
Hear not the fiends, that round him throng!
Of curtained rooms and firesides tell,
Bid Fancy work her genial spell,
That wraps in marvel and delight
December's long tempestuous night;
Makes courtly groups in summer bowers
Dance through pale Winter's midnight hours;
And July's eve its rich glow shed
On the hoar wreath, that binds his head;
Or knights on strange adventure bent,
Or ladies into thraldom sent;
Whatever gaiety ideal
Can substitute for troubles real.

Then let the storms of Winter sing,
And his sad veil the Snow-Fiend fling,
Though wailing lays are in the wind,
They reach not then the 'tranced mind;
Nor murky form, nor dismal sound
May pass the high, enchanted bound!

AN

ANCIENT BEECH-TREE.

IN THE PARK, AT KNOLE.

___

THE WOODLAND NYMPH.

___

Down in yon glade, that points to the red West,
O'erhung with ancient groves, whose shadows fall
So darkly on the ground, that the green moss
Is hardly known beneath them ;—in yon glade,
Just where the trees irregularly part
In long perspective, and an evening scene
Of sylvan grandeur glimmers, stands a beech,
Like some gigantic sentinel, advanced
On watch to guard the pass to sacred haunts.
Approach, and let thy nobler mind prevail ;
And, as thine eye measures its form, its large
Grey limbs upstretching in the air, among

The pendent, rich, luxuriant foliage,
Over the silvery rind, moss-mottled, showing
Like gleams of light 'mid their green shadows; if
Grace and grandeur ever touched thine heart, adore
And weep—weep tears of deep delight, and tears
Of gratitude, that thou canst weep such tears!

If thou would'st see in full magnificence
This canopy, most surely the domain
Of some lone Dryad,—come when Evening casts
Her yellow light, and gives its lower shades
Their most luxuriant tinge; speak not, but watch
And thou 'lt see haply at this dewy hour
The Nymph of this deep shade 'rise from her sleep.
The scared hind, bounding athwart the glades,
Springs not so lightly, nor so graceful turns,
When, listening to the step, that startles her,
She bends her slender neck and branched head
And shows her dark eyes, bright and innocent.

Oh, Nymph of graces, playful as these boughs,
When gentle airs play o'er them, thee I know,

And have, at eve, beheld thy dance of joy
In the proud shade, that shields thee from the storm,
And guards thy slumbers from the summer rain.
Thy noon-tide slumbers, too, I have beheld,
And the high canopy of boughs bespread,
When, laid in peace upon the twilight moss,
Where the green shadows deep and coolest fall,
Thy fairy court watched round thee—court of Elves,
That dwell unseen within the hollow leaves
Or inmost foliage, rocked by summer sighs.
These have I seen around thy mossy couch,
Fanning thy slumber with long leaves of lilies,
Scattering the white bells in thy twisted hair,
And binding each dark lock with wreaths of flowers.
Thy footsteps trod the tender hyacinth,
Blue and transparent as the light of Morn,
The dark-eyed violet, that weeps perfume,
The wild-rose tinted with the Dawn's first blush,
And sparkling with the tears and smiles she shed,
When, scattered from her hand, it fell to earth.

This ancient beech, this sylvan wonder, triumphs

Over the oak, whose spreading pomp has crowned
    him
King o' the woods; but his magnificence
Is rude and heavy,—while this lonely beech,
With all its wealth of green, transparent shadows,
(A graceful hill of leaves in the blue air,)
Still must be hailed the hero of the forest!

SEA-VIEWS.

MIDNIGHT.

CAROLLING sweetly to the midnight gale
Above the strife of waves, his voice is heard—
The sea-boy's voice, who, on some top-sail yard,
Bows with the mast, and hangs amid the clouds,
Or sweeps the salt foam from the billow's ridge,
And mocks its fury.   Far around he sees,
Beneath the night-gloom, ocean's wondrous fires
Flashing from surge to surge—a boding light,
That seems the spirit of the troubled realm.
Palely it gleams, though bright, now near, now dis-
    tant,
Shapeless, though visible — though threatening,
    mute :
Still, sweet he carols on the dizzy cap.

Anon, he hears the storm-bird's slender cry,
And scarcely marks her flitting round and round
And sheltering in the shrouds.   Oh, fearful bird!
Herald of warring winds! *he heeds thee not;*
Nor yet those hollow sounds from strand unseen;
Nor e'en those sullen lights among the clouds,
Whose hue they show more livid; for, behold!
Like to a star, which in th' horizon dawns,
There gleam those guiding, ever watchful fires,
Placed on some low peninsula's long line,
Or on some promontory's pointed horn,
And spied far on the solitary waves
By the poor mariner, who, rocked upon
His dark and billowy cradle, thinks of home,
His little cabin, sheltered by the cliff,
His blazing hearth, bright through the casement seen,
And all the dear-loved faces shining round;
And knows the smiles of welcome ambushed there.

Still cheerly sings the watch-boy; down he goes
Through gasping seas; now driving down the gulph,
Now rising light in air; while nearer roll

The thunders of the shore, reverbed from caves
Surge-worn, and cliffs high arching o'er the tide.
But now the plunging lead is heard, and now
The sullen voice of one below calls out
The sounded fathoms; then the master bids
His last sail furl; for well-known sands are nigh,
And louder sweeps the gale.   At last, he *nears*
Those friendly beacon fires, the level line
Of distance changes for the rugged shores,
Whose tops the horizontal twilight mark;
Soon they rise up more bold, solemn, distinct;
And wide unfolds the hospitable bay,
On whose deep margin spreads the wished-for port,
With many dim lamps quivering in the blast.
No joyful shout hails th' approaching crew;
For Sleep has waved his potent wand on high!
The lonely pier receives them; on they steer
For quiet depth, and gradually steal
Into the silent harbour—silent save
The drowsy rippling of the faint sea-tide,
Or when the watch-dog, on some neighbouring deck,
His honest vigil barks, as strangers pass.

And now each heart beats joyfully, as drops
The ready anchor; busy footsteps sound;
Loud swells the mingled voice; the narrow plank
Is hoisted and extends a tottering bridge,
That bears them to the quay; there, bounding light.
Once more they press the firm earth, and once more
Each to his long-left home in safety goes.
Dark is the way and silent; yet awhile
And an awakening voice shall call up hope,
And all the poor man's wealth, the wealth of heart!

TO THE SWALLOW.

O HAPPY bird! thy gay return I hail;
  For now I see young Spring, with all her train
Of sports and joys, borne on the western gale,
  And hear afar her sweetly warbling strain.

Once more the opening clouds shall now disclose
  The heaven's blue vault—the sun's all-cheering
      ray;
The vales, once more, in tender green repose,
  The violet wake beneath the breath of May.

O happy bird! how playful and how light
  Thy circling pinions skim the upward air;
Exulting, gay and playful in thy flight,
  Companion of the Summer season fair!

Yet, while I welcome thee, and wish thee long,
   I sigh to think that ere the Autumn fade,
Thou 'lt seek, in other climes, a vernal song,
   More gentle gales and renovated shade.

Ev'n now I see thee on the light clouds soar,
   And melt in distant æther from my view;
As laughing Summer, to the western shore,
   Over the seas Biscayan you pursue.

Thy policy to us, ah! dost thou lend?
Flies thus, with gay prosperity—the friend?

FOREST LAWNS.

Oh, forest lawns!—Oh, lawns of tender green,
That spread in sunshine, crowned with copsy groves,
Or, winding in deep glades, retire among
The shades of ages, my glad steps receive!
Oh! let me, with your fawns, bound o'er these
      slopes,
Fresh with the dew, that melts apace before
The morning ray, leaving long level lines
Of hoary silver, 'mid the various hues
Of lichen, turf and mead-flower. Let me seek,
With tempered pace and reverential thought,
Your far-seen solitudes and deepest gloom,
And often note the monarch of the woods
In pious wonder. Oh, ye stern-browed oaks,

That raise your giant arms on all the scene,
How like your parent Druids ye appear!
Lonely, severe and in your grandeur dark,
Your fearful shades, like superstitious night,
Fall on the awe-struck spirit! — — —
Steadfast ye stand, and ever silent, save
Unto the potent, unknown winds, that shake
Your grey tops, when a voice of plaint is heard.
The traveller, listening this, at even-tide,
Thinks 'tis the voice of one departed hence,
Prophet of evil, warning him of death!
Then to his fancy lours, with deeper gloom,
The cloud, which sheds a pale and ghastly light
Upon the woods.   He pauses oft, and back
Through the long forest-glades marks the last gleam
The sun has left, far in the lonely West;
While shapes uncertain seem to glide athwart
The twilight vista, and approach his path;
The hollow murmur swells upon his ear!
And, shuddering then, he takes his onward way.

How oft, ye Druid oaks!——
Your voice has sounded, in a distant age,

To him, who hears no more ; and now it speaks
In the same tone to him, who then was not—
The passing traveller of the living hour !
Thus, ever and anon, it sounds the knell
Of fleeting, swift mortality !

ON THE

RONDEAU,

"JUST LIKE LOVE IS YONDER ROSE."

———

No, ah! no; not just like love,
  Is yon gay and conscious rose;
  All its flaunting leaves disclose
Sun-shine joy—and fearless prove;
                  Not like love!
But yonder little violet-flower,
  That, folded in its purple veil,
  And trembling to the lightest gale,
Weeps beneath that shadowing bower,
                Is just like love!
Though filled with dew its closing eyes,
  Though bends its slender stem in air,
  It breathes perfume and blossoms fair,
It feeds on tears, and lives on sighs,
                Just like love!

And should a sun-beam kiss its leaf,
 How bright the dew-drops would appear !
 Like beams of hope upon a tear,
Like light of smiles through parting grief !
     And just like love !

DECEMBER'S EVE,

ABROAD.

———

AWFUL is Winter's setting sun,
  When, from beneath a sullen cloud,
He eyes his dreary course now run,
  And shrinks within his lurid shroud—

Leaving to Twilight's cold, grey sky
  Yon Minster's dark and lonely tower,
That seems to shun the searching eye,
  And vanish with the parting hour.

Dim is the long roof's sloping line,
  Whose airy pinnacles I trace,
Point over point, and o'er the shrine
  And eastern window's gothic grace.

While loud the winds, in chorus clear,
  Swell, or in sinking murmurs grieve,
The Ministers of Night I hear
  In requiem o'er December's Eve.

Wide o'er the plains and distant wolds
  I see her pall of darkness flow;
And all around, in mighty folds,
  Her winding sheet of new-fallen snow.

Farewell December's dismal night!
  Appalled I hear thy shrieking breath;
And view, aghast, by glimmering light,
  Thy visage, terrible in death!
Farewell December's dismal night!

DECEMBER'S EVE,

AT HOME.

WELCOME December's cheerful night,
  When the taper-lights appear ;
When the piled hearth blazes bright,
  And those we love are circled there !

And, on the soft rug basking lies,
  Outstretched at ease, the spotted friend,
With glowing coat and half-shut eyes,
  Where watchfulness and slumber blend.

Welcome December's cheerful hour,
  When books, with converse sweet combined,
And music's many-gifted power
  Exalt, or soothe th' awakened mind.

Then, let the snow-wind shriek aloud,
  And menace oft the guarded sash,
And all his diapason crowd,
  As o'er the frame his white wings dash.

He sings of darkness and of storm,
  Of icy cold, and lonely ways;
But, gay the room, the hearth more warm,
  And brighter is the taper's blaze.

Then, let the merry tale go round,
  And airy songs the hours deceive;
And let our heart-felt laughs resound,
  In welcome to December's Eve!

A SEA-VIEW.

A BREEZE is springing up.   Mark yon grey cloud,
That from th' horizon piles it's Alpy steeps
Upon the sky; there the fierce tempest rides.
Our vessel owns the gale, and all her sails
Are full; the broad and slanted deck cuts with i
    edge
The foaming waves, that roll almost within it,
And often bow their curling tops, as if
In homage.   Not so the onward billows;
For while, with steady force, the vexing prow
Flings wide the groaning waters, high rise they,
Darting their dragon-headed vengeance: now
Baffled they burst on either side with rage,
And dash their spray in the hard seaman's face.

The gale is rising : and the roughening waves
Show darker shades of green, with, here and there,
Far out, white foamy tops, that rise and fall
Incessant.   Storm-lights, issuing from the clouds,
Mark distances upon the mighty deep ;
There, in one gleam, a white sail scuds along—
Farther, those vessels seem to hang in shade ;
And, farther still, on the last edge of ocean,
Where falls a paler, mistier sun-light,
See where some port-town peeps above the tide,
With its long, level ramparts, turret-crowned ;
There a broad tower and there a slender spire
Stand high upon the light, while all between,
Of intermingled roofs, embattled gates,
Quays, ancient halls and smoking chimneys,—sunk
Low, and all blended in one common mass,
Are undiscerned so far.   There, all is calm ;
The waters slumber ; the anchored keels repose ;
And not a top-mast trembles ;——
While here the chafing billows mount the deck
Dash through the sturdy shrouds, and with their
      foam

Buffet the braced sail.   Toward that port
Our vessel steers, which from the seas and winds
May soon receive us. — — —
But ah! while yet we gaze, the vision fades!
The high-piled ramparts, overtopped with turrets,
Vanish in shade before the searching eye,
Which nought but waves and sky can trace o'er all
The lone horizon!   So on Calabria's shore,
Where the old Reggio spreads its walls
Beside the sea, the fairy's wand, at eve,
Is lifted—and behold! far on the waters,
Another landscape rise!*   Wood-mantled steeps
And shadowy mountains soar, and turrets from
Some promontory's point hang o'er the vale,
Where sleeps among its palms the hamlet low,
Hid from the bustling, ostentatious world,
Deep in the bosom of this silent scene.

Ah! beauteous work of Fairie! that can paint

* This phænomenon is noticed in Swinburne's Travels in
the Two Sicilies.   The people of Reggio attribute it, all natural as it is, to the fairy Morgana, and run with shouts to
the shore, to witness her wonders.

Unreal visions to th' admiring eye,
Charming it with distinct, though faithless forms.
The magic sceptre dropt, behold, they vanish !
A desert world of water's only there !

    •   •   •   •   •

And thus th' enchantress on the daily path
Of Youth attends, known only by her power
Unseen, and conjures up Hope, Joy and Bliss,
To dance in the fresh bowers of fadeless spring.
At Reason's touch the airy dream dissolves ;
We gaze, and wonder at such wild delusion,
Yet weep its loss, and court its forms again.
Hail, beauteous scenes of Fairie, Fancy's world !
Where Truth, so cold and colourless, comes not,
Or far away in lonely grandeur stands,
Like the great snowy Alps, whose cloudy shapes
And aspect stern (deforming the horizon),
Make the still landscape, spread below, appear
More green, more gay, more cheering to our view.
Hail, beauteous scenes of Fairie, Fancy's world !
And now, as if the spell had worked again,
The stormy shade far distant floats away.

Again the spired city shines in light,
Peering beyond the waves, here shadowed yet
By the lingering storm. The pier outstretches
Its arm to meet us, and the light-house shows
Its column, and we see the lanthorn high,
Suspended o'er the margin of the tide,
The star of the night-wandering mariner.
Hail, cheering port, first vision of the land,
Vision, but not illusion, hail again!

HAYLEY'S LIFE OF COWPER.

———

OH speak no more of Fiction's painted woes!
  Her laboured scenes are colourless and cold;
Her high-wrought sorrows are but dull repose,
  Beside the tale that simple Truth has told.

O'er the sad Poet dead shall Pity weep,
  Weep tears of anguish, such as mothers shed
O'er the poor infant, when its paling lip
  Moves with a last faint smile; when droops the
    head,

And the imploring eyes look up once more
  To her, whose fondness can no aid dispense!
'Tis well there is a Higher World, where soar
  The accepted hopes of suffering Innocence!

WRITTEN IN THE ISLE OF WIGHT.

Oh! for a cottage on the shady brow
Of this green Island, where the Channel flows
With less tumultuous wave, and sends abroad
The many sails of England to the world,
And beareth to his home the mariner,
Who shouts to view the light blue hills, that dawn
O'er Wight's gay plains; and soon he spies the
    woods,
That shade its shores, and brighter tints of corn
And pastoral slopes and all their " green delights."
Advancing gently, 'mid the sleepy tide,
Soon he marks some long-left object clear,
A lofty watch-tower, or some village church,
Or the white parsonage peeping through the trees,
To which, when last beheld, he sighed farewell

With throbbing grief.—These now he hails with joy,
As he steers onward to the well-known shore.

Oh! for a cottage on the breezy cliff,
That points the crescent of thy harbour, Cowes!
And bears the raptured glance o'er seas and shores—
A boundless prospect, tinted all around
With summer shades of soft ethereal blue!—
O'er the wide waters rise the far-famed downs
Of Sussex; while thy forests, Hampshire, vast,
Spread their dark line, for many a winding mile,
By the blue waves, till, failing, the sight rests
Where yon dim hill-tops overlook the main.
There Purbeck's summits rise, while broader hills,
Marking their grey lines on the forest shade,
Lead back the eye to where Southampton's vale
Pours forth th' abundant wave, and spreads its
        lawns,
Its jutting slopes, with villas gaily crowned,
Its sheltered cots, the rough wood's shade, whence
        peers
The village fane 'mid the high foliage :—

Southampton's vale, where lurks the twilight glade,
Whose ancient oaks their branches stretch austere,
And half conceal that Abbey's fretted arch,
As if to guard from eye and hand profane
The mouldering stones, whose pious founder once
Dropped them, green acorns, in this hallowed ground,
To shelter and adorn the sainted walls,
Whose long-forgotten sons mused 'neath their shade,
Blest thoughts of sure Eternity; and now
Leave here all that was mortal of themselves.
Oh! reverence this ground; for it is holy,
Sacred to pious thought; for worldly grace
By the high-gifted poet often praised.
Here winged steps have passed, and brightest
        thoughts,
Creative as the sun-beam, have up-flown.
Here pensive Gray some sad sweet moments passed,
And breathed a spell that saved these falling walls;
There walks that solemn vision*, telling his beads;
Where 'neath the leafy gloom, the Poet's glance

---

* "In the bosom of the woods (concealed from profane eyes)
lie the ruins of Nettley Abbey; there may be richer and
greater houses, but the abbot is content with his situation.

Espied him! Still athwart yon vista dark
Shoots the white sail; still in the sun the waves
Glitter, as when Gray's musing abbot viewed them,
Measuring the moments with his pangs. Oh! pause
Awhile, and shed a melancholy tear
To the departed shade of him, who sung
" The paths of glory lead but to the grave:"
Weep o'er the memory of that wondrous Bard,
That master of the song, whose full-toned harp
Called round him loftiest themes of Fantasy,
Whose voice, rolling on the midnight thunder,
Waked sublimest awe; or played in cadence,
While the Graces danced; or, still oftener, mourned
O'er mortal doom and life's brief vanities,
While early youth and all the train of joy
Would leave their sports, listening the strain that
      bade
Them woo the languishments of Melancholy.

See there, at the top of that hanging meadow, under the
shade of those old trees that bend into a half circle about it,
he is walking slowly, and bidding his beads for the souls of
his benefactors, interred in that venerable pile, that lies beneath him." Letter of Mr. Gray to Mr. Nichols, Nov. 19,
1764.—Mason's Life of Gray, p. 381.

Farewell ! thou mighty master, who, with high
Disdain of vulgar fame, " knew thine own worth
And reverenced the lyre," and kept thy still
Footstep far away from the thronged path and
Vanity's dull round.   Farewell! thou doff'st
Thy mortal weeds, and the same strain sublime,
That moralized th' unstoried lives and deaths
Of villagers, is oft repeated o'er thy grave,
With faltering voice, by those, who walk thy path
From Eton's shades to Stoke, and view the scene
That filled thy youthful eye and charmed thy mind—
Where, years ago, thy " careless childhood strayed,
A stranger yet to pain." — — —

Now let us leave the vale, thus dedicate
To memory, sweet and melancholy,
And trace the landscape o'er yon chalky ridge
To Portsdown, shielding in its concave all
That tract of greyer land, that banks the sea.
On the low point extends the busy port,
Its forts and ramparts rising o'er the main,
And wide o'erlooking all its anchored fleets.

Oh! for the magic pencil of Lorraine!
To give the soft perspective, where the waves
Fade to thin air in tints of mildest blue,
And the dark masts and cobweb-shrouds and lines
Of spiry shipping trace themselves in light.

Midway the sails of various vessels swell,
Gliding their silent course; here the swift-winged
Slant cutter skims the sea; and there the skiff,
Low on the mighty waters, shows a speck,
Invisible, but that its tiny sail
Catches the sunbeam, and, wondrous! tells that
Human life dwells in the moving atom
Amidst the waters.   While we gaze, each wave
Threatens to whelm it; and the shores appear
Too distant for its small and feeble wing;
Yet on it goes in safety, and displays
Regular purpose, well-considered rules,
And skill, which guides its weakness through the
    strength
Of waves, o'er pathless distance, to the sheltering
    port.

Oh! that the old Spirit of Song
Would sound his harp from this high aery brow,
And bid its sweet tones languish, till the Nymphs,
That dwell beneath its waves, wake at the strain,
And send up answering music, now scarce heard,
Now lost, now heard again with wondering doubt,
Till, rising slow, a clearer chorus swells
In the soft gale, and makes its voice its own :
Then, the full sounds float over woods and rocks ;
And then, descending on the wave, retire,
Die with the 'plaining of the distant tide,
And leave a blessed peace o'er all the soul.

Raise such a strain, O Nymphs! whose spell may
        spread
A sweeter grace on all the eye beholds,
That the fine vision of these seas and shores
May paint their living colours on the mind,
With charm so forceful, as Time cannot fade.
Then Memory with their own truth shall give
The blue shades of the main, under these dark
And waving boughs upon the steep ; the mast

Now seen, or lost, in the smooth bay, as choose
The dancing leaves ; the grey fort on the strand,
Its low, round tower o'ercanopied with elms,
The pacing sentinel, beneath their gloom,
Safe from the noon-day sun. Then would she paint
The slopes, that swell beside thy harbour, Cowes,
With pasture gay and oft with groves embrowned,
That amid veiling leaves, half show the villa,
Gay mimic of a cottage, or the trim crest
Of some proud castle, falsely old. Thy town
Would still be seen to climb the craggy bank ;
Thy vale, withdrawing from the sunny bay,
Would wind beneath these green hills' shade, where droops
The sail becalmed, that on Medina's tide
Bears the full freight to Newport. Memory then
Would give these nearer scenes of gentle beauty,
Those spreading waters and the dim-seen coast,
Fading into the sky. Then, gentle Nymphs,
Borne far upon the winds, my song might tell
Of your sweet haunts, perchance in Indian seas—
Of them, who dance before the rising sun,
With songs of joyance breathing spicy gales.

Methinks, I hear their far-off notes complain:
" Oh ! ne'er yet tripp'd we on the yellow sands,
That Fame says base the cliffs of English land ;
Never yet danced we on those heights, that send
Airs from their mantling woods ; never yet trod
The ridges of her stormy waves, nor watched
The tender azure melt into the green,
Then deepen to the purple's changing shades,
Beneath the sleepy indolence of noon.
For such delights we 'll leave our splendid clime,
Our groves of cassia and our coral bowers,
Our diamond-beaming caves and golden beds,
'Broidered with rubies, with transparent pearl,
And emeralds, that steal the sea-wave's hue,
And shells of rainbow-tint, fairy pavilions :
All but our tortoise cars ; they shall bear us
O'er many a curling surge and chasm deep,
Farther than where the blended sea and sky
Hide from our sight the cooler, better oceans.
That way seek we those temperate islands, now
Wearing green Neptune's livery, crowned with oak,
And terraced with bright cliffs ; such Oberon,

The fairy, told of, to win our music.
'Twas a charmful moon-time, and he perched him
In a purple shell, he called his mantle,
And basked him in the pure light, and then asked
A lullaby to soothe his care, for he
Was sad and weary, and had, all the day,
Toiled on a north-beam ; and now Titania,
For whom he sought, had left the spicy steeps
Of India, on a bat's wing, at twilight.
We asked a story of the northern clime
To pay our melody, and I remember
It told of castles moving on the waves,
Of a soft emerald throne upon an isle,
Beyond the falling sun, and other wonders,
That we, all night, could well have listened him,
But that he craved our pity and our song.
On that we breathed a soul into our shells,
And charmed him into slumber !"

SONNET

TO THE LARK.

———

SWEET lark! I hear thy thrilling note on high,
  The note of rapture, that thy bosom pours
To Spring's fresh gales, green plains and azure sky,
  As o'er the mountains steal Morn's blushing hours.
With silent step they come and meekened grace,
  In twilight's veil half-hid from mortal view,
Wafting rich fragrance through the crystal space,
  O'er groves and valleys shedding April dew.
Gay bird! now all the woods in silence sleep,
  How sweet thy music comes upon the air,
And dies at distance, as, up heaven's blue steep,
  Thou, lessening, soar'st to meet Aurora's star!
Oh! bird of hope and joy, thou point'st the way
  That I would go—high o'er life's cloudy day!

ON READING THE FOLLOWING BEAUTIFUL LINES, WRITTEN BY THE LATE LADY ELIZABETH LEE, SISTER OF EARL HARCOURT, IN A BOWER CALLED BY HER NAME, AT ST. LEONARD'S HILL, THE SEAT OF THE EARL, IN WINDSOR FOREST; A SEAT WHICH STRANGERS ARE SOMETIMES PERMITTED TO VIEW.

" This peaceful shade—this green-roofed bower,
   GREAT MAKER ! all are full of Thee ;
Thine is the bloom, that decks the flower,
   And Thine the fruit, that bends the tree.

As much Creative Goodness charms
   In these low shrubs, that humbly creep,
As in the oak, whose giant-arms
   Wave o'er the high romantic steep.

The bower, the shade, retired, serene,
   The grateful heart may most affect ;
Here, GOD in every leaf is seen,
   And man has leisure to reflect !

"AND I TOO WAS ONCE OF ARCADIA."

FROM this high lawn, beneath the varied green
   Of grove and bower, dark oak and blossomed
      shade,
How brightly spreads the vale ! how grand the scene
   Of forest woods and towers, that lift the head

Majestic from the strife of ages past !
  And seem to view, with melancholy smile,
The gloom of thought by solemn Pity cast
  On the world, fleeting to its rest ;—the while

The fleeting world, all various and gay,
  Sports in those villas and those hamlets free,
Where stretching tints of ripened harvest play
  Among dark woods and meads of Arcady.

There Spires of Peace arise, and straw-roofed farm
  By village green, from 'mid it's antient grove
Sends the high curling smoke, renowned charm
  Of those, who watch how lights and shadows rove.

Embattled Windsor, throned upon the vale,
  Beneath these boughs displays its bannered state ;
And learned Eton, o'er its willows pale,
  Looks stern and sad, as mourning Henry's fate.

On this high lawn, where Nature's wealth we view,
  All is instinct with life and fine delight !

Trees of all shades, the flowers of every hue,
  Shrubs breathing joy* and blooming on the sight.

Here bliss may dwell, and never, never die!
  Vain thought! in that low bower there seems a
      voice,
Breathed, soft as summer winds o'er waters sigh,
  " I once, like you, could in this scene rejoice.

This was my bower of bliss! Approach and read!"
  It sunk, that solemn sound, and died on air.
Within the cell I passed with reverend dread,
  And found the angel-spirit still was there.

Still in "that green-roofed bower," that "peaceful
      shade,"
  Whose changeful prospect seems for ever new,
The pomp of forests stretching till they fade,
  And sleep in softness on the distant blue.—

* The delicious fragrance of the mangolia, which flou-
rishes in great abundance before the colonnade, fills the
breakfast-room, and scents all the upper part of the lawn.
Its bushes are wide and high, its egg-flowers large, and its
foliage broad and glossy, like a bay-leaf.

Still in that fine repose—that once-loved bower,
　Breathe thoughts of heavenly mind, that speak
　　　of GOD !
And tell a heart, which, grateful, owned His power
　In every leaf, that paints the humble sod.

Fast fell my tears, as flowed with her's my thought,
　The living feeling with the voice of Death !
'The glowing joy by Nature's beauty wrought
　With proof how transient is even rapture's breath.

Here in this shade she sat ! fast fell my tears ;
　When my sad mind a hushing music won ;
Again mild accents seemed to soothe my fears,
　And murmur, " Grieve not that her race is run !

The pious heart, the comprehensive mind,
　These were of Heaven, and are to Heaven re-
　　　turned !"
It was a seraph's voice upon the wind ;
　I heard her song of joy ; I heard ! nor longer
　　　mourned.

TO THE RIVER DOVE.

Oh ! stream beloved by those,
  With Fancy who repose,
And court her dreams 'mid scenes sublimely wild,
  Lulled by the summer-breeze,
  Among the drowsy trees
Of thy high steeps, and by thy murmurs mild,

  My lonely footsteps guide,
  Where thy blue waters glide,
Fringed with the Alpine shrub and willow light;
  'Mid rocks and mountains rude,
  Here hung with shaggy wood,
And there upreared in points of frantic height.

Beneath their awful gloom,
Oh! blue-eyed Nymph, resume
The mystic spell, that wakes the poet's soul!
While all thy caves around
In lonely murmur sound,
And feeble thunders o'er these summits roll.

O shift the wizard scene
To banks of pastoral green
When mellow sun-set lights up all thy vales;
And shows each turf-born flower,
That, sparkling from the shower,
Its recent fragrance on the air exhales.

When Evening's distant hues
Their silent grace diffuse
In sleepy azure o'er the mountain's head;
Or dawn in purple faint,
As nearer cliffs they paint,
Then lead me 'mid thy slopes and woodland shade.

Nor would I wander far,
When Twilight lends her star,

And o'er thy scenes her doubtful shades repose ;
　　Nor when the Moon's first light
　　Steals on each bowery height,
Like the winged music o'er the folded rose.

　　Then, on thy winding shore,
　　The fays and elves, once more,
Trip in gay ringlets to the reed's light note ;
　　Some launch the acorn's *ring*,
　　Their sail—Papilio's wing,
Thus shipped, in chace of moon-beams, gay they
　　　float.

　　But, at the midnight hour,
　　I woo thy thrilling power,
While silent moves the glow-worm's light along,
　　And o'er the dim hill-tops
　　The gloomy red moon drops,
And in the grave of darkness leaves thee long.

　　Even then thy waves I hear,
　　And own a nameless fear,
As, 'mid the stillness, the night winds do swell,

Or (faint from distance) hark
To the lone watch-dog's bark!
Answering a melancholy far sheep bell.

O! Nymph fain would I trace
Thy sweet awakening grace,
When summer dawn first breaks upon thy stream;
And see thee braid thy hair;
And keep thee ever there,
Like thought recovered from an antique dream!

THE SEA-MEW.

───

FORTH from her cliffs sublime the sea-mew goes
To meet the storm, rejoicing! To the woods
She gives herself; and, borne above the peaks
Of highest head-lands, wheels among the clouds,
And hears Death's voice in thunder roll around,
While the waves far below, driven on the shore,
Foaming with pride and rage, make hollow moan.
Now, tossed along the gale from cloud to cloud,
She turns her silver wings touched by the beam,
That through a night of vapours darts its long,
Level line; and, vanishing 'mid the gloom,
Enters the secret region of the storm;
But soon again appearing, forth she moves
Out from the mount'nous shapes of other clouds,

And, sweeping down them, hastens to new joys.
It was the wailing of the deep she heard !
No fears repel her : when the tumult swells,
Ev'n as the spirit-stirring trumpet glads
The neighing war-horse, is the sound to her.
O'er the waves hovering, while they lash the rocks,
And lift, as though to reach her, their chafed tops,
Dashing the salt foam o'er her downy wings,
Higher she mounts, and from her feathers shakes
The shower, triumphant.   As they sink, she sinks,
And with her long plumes sweeps them in their fall,
As if in mockery ; then, as they retreat,
She dances o'er them, and with her shrill note
Dares them, as in scorn.

It is not thus she meets their summer smiles ;
Then, skimming low along the level tide,
She dips the last point of her crescent wings,
At measured intervals, with playful grace,
And rises, as retreating to her home.
High on yon 'pending rock, but poised awhile
In air, as though enamoured of the scene,

She drops, at once, and settles on the sea.
On the green waves, transparent then she rides,
And breathes their freshness, trims her plumage,
　　white;
And, listening to the murmur of the surge,
Doth let them bear her wheresoe'er they will.

Oh! bird beloved of him, who, absent long
From his dear native land, espies thee ere
The mountain tops o'er the far waters rise,
And hails thee as the harbinger of home!
Thou bear'st to him a welcome on thy wings.
His white sail o'er th' horizon thou hast seen
And hailed it, with thy oft-repeated cry,
Announcing England. "England is near!" he cries,
And every seaman's heart an echo beats,
And "England—England!" sounds along the deck,
Mounts to the shrouds, and finds an answering
　　voice,
Ev'n at the top-mast head, where, posted long,
The "look out" sailor clings, and with keen eye,
By long experience finely judging made,

Reads the dim characters of air-veiled shores.
O happy bird! whom Nature's changing scenes
Can ever please; who mount'st upon the wind
Of Winter and amid the grandeur soar'st
Of tempests, or sinkest to the peaceful deep,
And float'st with sunshine on the summer calm!
O happy bird! lend me thy pinions now.
Thy joys are mine, and I, like thee, would skim
Along the pleasant curve of the salt bays,
Where the blue seas do now serenely sleep;
Or, when they waken to the Evening breeze,
And every crisping wave reflects her tints
Of rose and amber,—like thee, too, would I
Over the mouths of the sea-rivers float,
Or watch, majestic, on the tranquil tide,
The proud ships follow one another down,
And spread themselves upon the mighty main,
Freighted for shores that shall not dawn on sight,
Till a new sky uplift its burning arch,
And half the globe be traversed. Then to him,
The home-bound seaman, should my joyous flight
Once more the rounding river point,—to him

Who comes, perchance, from coasts of darkness,
    where
Grim Ruin, from his throne of hideous rocks,
O'ercanopied with pine, or giant larch,
Scowls on the mariner, and Terror wild
Looks through the parting gloom with ghastly eye,
Listens to woods, that groan beneath the storm,
And starts to see the river-cedar fall.

How sweet to him, who from such strands returns,
How sweet to glide along his homeward stream
By well-known meads and woods and village cots,
That lie in peace around the ivied spire
And ancient parsonage, where the small, fresh
    stream
Gives a safe haven to the humbler barks
At anchor, just as last be viewed the scene.
And soft as then upon the surface lies
The sunshine, and as sweet the landscape
Smiles, as on that day he sadly bade farewell
To those he loved.   Just so it smiles, and yet
How many other days and months have fled,

What shores remote his steps have wandered o'er,
What scenes of various life unfolded strange,
Since that dim yesterday ! The present scene
Unchanged, though fresh, appears the only truth,
And all the interval a dream ! May those
He loves still live, as lives the landscape now ;
And may to-morrow's sun light the thin clouds
Of doubt with rainbow-hues of hope and joy !

Bird ! I would hover with thee o'er the deck,
Till a new tide with thronging ships should tremble ;
Then, frightened at their strife, with thee I 'd fly
To the free waters and the boundless skies,
And drink the light of heaven and living airs ;
Then with thee haunt the seas and sounding shores,
And dwell upon the mountain's beaked top,
Where nought should come but thou and the wild
    winds.
There would I listen, sheltered in our cell,
The tempest's voice, while midnight wraps the world.
But, if a moon-beam pierced the clouds, and shed
Its sudden gleam upon the foaming waves,

Touching with pale light each sharp line of cliff,
Whose head towered darkly, which no eye could
    trace,—
Then downward I would wheel amid the storm,
And watch, with untired gaze, the embattled surges
Pouring in deep array, line after line,
And hear their measured war-note sound along
The groaning coast, whereat the winds above
Answer the summons, and each secret cave,
Untrod by footsteps, and each precipice,
That oft had on the unconscious fisher frowned,
And every hollow bay and utmost cape
Sighs forth a fear for the poor mariner.
He, meanwhile, hears the sound o'er waters wide ;
Lashed to the mast, he hears, and thinks of home.

    O bird ! lend me thy wings,
That swifter than the blast I may out-fly
Danger, and from yon port the life-boat call.
And see ! e'en now the guardian bark rides o'er
The mountain-billows, and descends through chasms
Where lurks Destruction eager for his prey,
With eyes of flashing fire and foamy jaws.

He, by strange storm-lights shown, uplifts his head,
And, from the summit of each rising wave,
Darts a grim glance upon the daring crew,
And sinks the way their little boat must go!
But she, with blessings armed, best shield! as if
Immortal, surmounts the abyss, and rides
The watery ridge upon her pliant oars,
Which conquer the wild, raging element
And that dark demon, with angelic power.
Wave after wave, he sullenly retreats,
With oft repeated menace, and beholds
The poor fisherman, with all his fellows,
Borne from his grasp in triumph to the shore—
There Hope stands watchful, and her call is heard
Wafted on wishes of the crowd. Hark! hark!
Is that her voice rejoicing? 'Tis her song
Swells high upon the gale, and 'tis her smile,
That gladdens the thick darkness. THEY ARE
    SAVED.

Bird of the winds and waves and lonely shores,
Of loftiest promontories—and clouds,

And tempests—Bird of the sun-beam, that seeks
Thee through the storm, and glitters on thy wings!
Bird of the sun-beam and the azure calm,
Of the green cliff, hung with gay summer plants,
Who lov'st to sit in stillness on the bough,
That leans far o'er the sea, and hearest there
The chasing surges and the hushing sounds,
That float around thee, when tall shadows tremble,
And the rock-weeds stream lightly on the breeze.
O bird of joy! what wanderer of air
Can vie with thee in grandeur of delights,
Whose home is on the precipice, whose sport
Is on the waves? O happy, happy bird!
Lend me thy wings, and let thy joys be mine!

TO THE WINDS.

SPIRIT! who dwellest in the secret clouds,
Unseen, unknown, yet heard o'er all the world!
Who reign'st in storms and darkness half the year,
Yet sometimes lov'st, in Summer's season bright,
To breathe soft music through her azure dome:
Oft heard art thou amongst the high tree-tops,
In mournful and so sweet a melody,
As though some Angel, touched with human grief,
Soothed the sad mind. Oh, viewless, viewless
     wind!
I love thy potent voice, whether in storms
It gives to thunder clouds their impulse dread,
Swells the Spring airs, or sighs in Autumn's groves,

Mourning the dying leaf.   Whate'er the note,
Thy power entrances, wins me from low cares,
And bears me towards GOD, who bids you breathe,
And bids the morning of a higher world
Dawn on my hopes.

MOONLIGHT.

A SCENE.

On the bright margin of Italia's shore,
  Beneath the glance of summer-noon we stray,
And, indolently happy, ask no more
  Than cooling airs, that o'er the ocean play;

And watch the bark, that, on the busy strand,
  Washed by the sparkling tide, awaits the gale,
Till, high among the shrouds, the sailor-band
  Gallantly shout, and raise the swelling sail.

On the broad deck a various group recline,
  Touched with the moonlight, yet half-hid in shade,
Who, silent, watch the bark the coast resign,
  The Pharos lessen, and the mountains fade.

We, indolently happy, ask alone
  · The wandering airs, which o'er the ocean stray,
To bring some sad Venetian sonnet's tone,
   From that lone vessel floating far away!

SMILES.

It was a smile—a fleeting smile,
   Like a faint gleam through Autumn's shade,
That softly, sweetly, did beguile,
   As it around her dimples played.

What are smiles, and whence their sway?
   Smiles that, o'er the features stealing,
To the gazer's heart convey
   All the varied world of feeling,
                        What are smiles?
Do they dwell in Beauty's eye?
   No! nor on her playing cheek,
Nor on her wavy lip—though nigh
   Seems the glancing charm they seek.
                        Where do they dwell?

Where?—Their home is in the mind;
  Smiles are light—the light of soul!
Light of many tints combined,
  And of strong and sure control.

                              Smiles are light.

There's a smile—the smile of Joy,
  Bright as glance of May's fresh morn;
And one, that gleams but to destroy,—
  'Tis the lightning smile of Scorn.

There is a smile of glow-worm hue,
  That glimmers not near scenes of Folly,
Pale and strange and transient too,—
  The smile of awful Melancholy.

Like to the sad and silvery showers,
  Falling in an April sun,
Is the smile, that Pity pours
  O'er the deed, that Fate has done.

Dear is Friendship's meeting look,
  As moonlight on a sleeping vale,

Soothing those the sun forsook—
  So does that o'er Care prevail.

But who the first pure tint has seen,
  That trembles on the edge of Morning,
When summer's veil is so serene,
  Hiding half and half adorning?

They, who this have seen, may know,
  What the smile that's here intended;
They, who do to Laura go,
  See that smile with beauty blended.

THE REED OF POESY.

Oh! sweet reed, come hither!
  Never from thee will I part;
For oft, like sun-shine weather,
  Thy music has cheered my heart:
                    Oh! sweet reed, come hither.
Many a forest-green mountain
  In leafless November I've seen;
Many a daisy-rimmed fountain
  In frozen December has been;

Many an April bower,
  And many a valley of May
Bright with sunbeam and flower,
  I've seen on a Winter's day.

Oft, in the depth of December,
   When the night-blast shrieked aloud,
And sadly bade me remember,
   That Death was abroad in his shroud ;

Thy welcomest note light sounding
   Has flattered my fears to rest ;
My lone, lone hearth surrounding
   With many a fairy guest.

And many a scene of wonder,
   Rising from forth the dark night,
In veil thrown but half asunder,
   Has thrilled me with dread delight.

How oft, in some measureless chamber,
   I have seen the traveller wait,
Through the dull night of December,
   All fearful of some sad fate.

And I 've heard that voice so hollow
   Break once on his startled ear ;

And seen him how sadly follow,
  And dimly disappear.

And, when the grey doubtful morning
  Has gleamed pale over the waste,
I 've viewed him all safe returning,
  And smiling at danger past.

So came, sweet reed, come hither!
  I never from thee will part;
For oft, like sunshine weather,
  Thy music has cheered my heart.
                Oh! sweet reed, come hither!

EDWY.

A POEM, IN THREE PARTS.

PART I.

THE HAZEL TREE.

A SUMMER SONG OF FAIRIE.

LIGHTLY green with springing buds,
 The hazel twines her fairy bowers,
In yon dell o'erhung with woods,
 Where the brook its music pours.

O'er the margin of the stream
 Peeps the yellow marygold,
And lilies, where the waters gleam,
 Bend their heads so fair and cold.

Know ye why the Elfin-band
 Watch beneath the hazel-bough?
'Tis to guard its MAGIC WAND
 And its blossoms, as they blow.

THESE, gathered at the mid-day hour,
 To mortal eyes their haunts betray;
THAT has the strange enchanting power
 To call up a prophetic Fay.

Be she down among the rills,
 In some wild-wood dingle hid;
Or dancing on the moonlight hills—
 She must speed, as she is bid.

Or sleep she on the mossy bed,
 Under the blossom-breathing lime,
That sheds sweet freshness over head—
 The freshness of the morning prime;

Or stray she with old Thames serene
 Through osier-tufts and lofty groves,

By royal towers, or cottaged green,
  Still must she leave what best she loves—

Leave the thatched cot, where finest spreads*
  The turf, 'mid every choicest flower,
And the far-branching chestnut sheds
  Over the wave its greenest shower.

Where, silver-streak'd, that polished wave
  Glides by with lingering, sweet farewell,
While stately swans their proud necks lave,
  And seem to feel some fairy spell.

Then marvel not that Elfins fair
  Guard the thin wand and hazel bloom;
Since these can all their haunts lay bare,
  By hidden stream, or forest gloom.

—Near Windsor's shades there dwelt a youth,
  Who fast was bound in Cupid's chain;

* The Princess Elizabeth's late cottage at Old Windsor.

But how to try his lady's truth
   By mortal means he sought in vain.

He to a chamber dim withdrew,
   Where serpent's skin and head of toad
Hinted of themes he must pursue,
   Ere secret would to him be showed.

It was a chamber magical,
   Where light in partial gleams appeared,
And showed strange shapes upon the wall,
   By his own mystic learning reared.

Thence to the hazel-copse he went,
   When the sun was flaming high;
And there the twining branches rent;
   For then no Fay was watching nigh.

Fast asleep in closed flowers,
   And all unheard, and all unseen,
Who, that walked these noontide bowers,
   Could guess that any Elves had been?—

Next, to the forest-hills he hied,
  To pull the wild thyme's budding bloom,
Fresh from some haunted dingle's side ;
  For, it must blow where Fairies come.

Just such a dingle still is seen,
  Hanging upon the Park's high brow,
Deep buried in the shadowy green,
  Where tall o'erarching beeches grow.

Here oft the Fairies revel keep,
  To bless the Castle's moonlight hours,
And peep, as winds these branches sweep,
  At Windsor diadem'd with towers.

Grass, that crowns a Fairie's throne,
  Marygolds—her canopy,
Lilies, for her cradle known,
  These he gathered, three and three.

Well prepared with hazel-leaves,
  Thus the wondrous charm distill,

Which, laid on an eye, that grieves,
   Shows each sprite of grove, or rill.

" Three hazel-wands peel smooth and white,
   Just a twelvemonth old—no more :
Thrice on each wand the full name write
   Of the Fay you would implore.

" Then in earth these wands consign ;
   In earth, that elfin footsteps tread,
Extract them with well-muttered line,
   Unheard of man—by man unread.

" Next, to the North your visage turn,
   Invoke her name, with thrice told three,
Be she by forest, mead, or bourne,
   Her on your magic glass you 'll see."

With shaking hand he peeled the wand ;
   Then would he trace her name, I wot ;
Edwy the Love-Fay would command ;
   But Edwy had her name forgot.

Full of great flaws to aught but love
   Is the memory of a lover;
Now he must watch where Fairies rove,
   Or this name he 'll ne'er recover.

Back o'er the sunny hills he goes
   To his green home in Windsor shades,
To draw the charm, that shall expose
   The Elfin-Court, when day-light fades.

Down by good Clewer's winding mead,
   And where the silver currents glide,
A plume of elms lifts high it's head,
   And casts it's shadow on the tide.

All dark and still the feathery grove
   Sleeps in the streamy light below;
The streamy light with placid love
   And hushing murmur seems to flow.

There Elves, 'twas said, in ringlets went,
   When chimes sang midnight to the land,

If then, on Windsor's battlement,
  Tip-toe the full-orbed Moon should stand.

Duly distilled the flowery charm,
  Thither Edway must repair,
And, that no check the spell might harm,
  Ere the sun-set he was there.

The golden tints of Evening lie
  Upon the smoothly-flowing stream,
Tint the old walls and turrets high,
  And lower on the wood-tops gleam.

And, slanting o'er the willowed vale,
  The blessed Henry's fane enshrined,
It's fretted windows, turrets pale,
  And pinnacles far ranged behind.

And now the soothing hour is come,
  The star-light hour, when all is still,
Save the far-distant village hum,
  And the lone watch-bark from the hill;

And wheels which, far-off travelling,
   Pass unseen in bowery lane,
Like to the sea-tide murmuring,
   Now loud and lost, then loud again.

He laid the charm upon his eyes,
   And looked with desperate courage round ;
Alas ! no tripping phantoms rise
   On the shadowy, Fairie ground.

Patience is a lover's duty !
   Here, counting every distant chime,
He exalts his lady's beauty,
   In quaint, or pity-moving rhime.

Till, in the East, a shadowy light,
   Rising behind the Castle-walls,
Gives the dim turrets to his sight,
   And in mute watch his spirit thralls.

As slow the unseen Moon ascends,
   More darkly drawn the towers appear,

Till every doubtful mass expands,
  And lives upon the radiant air;

Then, peers she o'er the broad Keep's height,
  A spreading curve of light serene;
And, faithful to her loved Midnight,
  There, reigns it's pale and pensive Queen.

And touches, with her silver ray,
  Terrace and woody steep below
The river's willow-sheltered bay,
  And waters quivering as they flow.

Where'er th' Enchantress points her wand,
  Forth from the deep of darkness crowd
Pale glimmering shapes, and silent stand
  As waked from Death's unfolding shroud.

The landscape lived, clear spread the lawn,
  The groves their shadowy tops unfurled,
And airy hills in prospect dawn,
  Like vision of another world.

The chimes sang midnight ; Edwy shook,
  While by the grove of elm he stood,
And cast a sly and wistful look
  Around the turf and o'er the flood.

That wrinkled flood, all silver bright,
  No sail of Fairie pinnace showed,
Nor, 'neath the still elm's bowery night,
  A glimpse of elfin-pageant glowed.

St. George's chimes, with falter sweet,
  Like infants, tried their task to say ;
But, waked from midnight's slumber meet,
  Th' imperfect accents died away.

And soft they sunk to sleep again,
  Ere the slow song was duly closed,
As seeming feebly to complain
  Of broken rest, e'en while they dozed.

But Fairies met not Edwy's eye ;
  For, here, alas ! no more they rove ;

Some urchins of the College nigh
   Had surely scared them from the grove ;

Such as the forest-keepers here
   Have followed, helter-skelter, round
Hills, woods and dales, for tracking deer ;
   Till fond Thames bore the wights to ground ;

To Eton ground, where, safe from law,
   And praising oft the helping tide,
They peeped, well hid in grass, and saw
   The foresters on t'other side !

Such as the May-pole* oft has watched
   Doff gown and mount the coach on high ;
Such as the tavern-dinner snatched,
   The bottle drank and ate the pie,

In fifteen minutes and away !
   And, if an oxen-herd they met,

* A Maypole formerly stood on the Green, before the
gates of the Long Walk at Windsor, where pranks of this
sort have often been played.

Sprung on their horns, in laughing play,
    Then gravely joined the school-room set.

Oh! those were happy times, I ween,
    The light of Morning o'er the sky—
That touches all the varied scene
    With life-full gleams of hope and joy:

The angered fairies, in revenge,
    Still, the tale goes, "their tyrants flout;"
Plunge them in scrapes and mischief strange,
    Then leave them to a flogging-bout!

But oft good Robin proves their friend,
    And lays his bandage on the eyes
Of the grave Heads, who mildly blend
    Remembrance with severe surmise.

And now, in more removed ground,
    Up in the high Park's ancient shade,
On the grey forest's lonely bound,
    These fairies dance in secret glade;

Where oaks Plantagenet still frown,
  Great Edward's tree e'en each appears,
A warlike ruin, gaunt and lone,
  The spectre of five hundred years.

Nursed by long centuries gone by,
  Reared in the storms, that wrecked their kings,
Oh ! could they give the Past a sigh,
  And speak the tale of vanished things,

The peopled scenes they have beheld,
  In long succession, varied guise,
More wonders here had stood revealed,
  Than aught, that Fairie dream supplies.

Thus Edwy, with a face of rue,
  Returned home for future feat ;
Thus he, who does adventure woo,
  Must sometimes disappointment meet.

PART II.

THE FAIRIE COURT.

——

——

EDWY, in his lonely chamber,
 Plying still his magic lore,
Watched, when all was hushed in slumber,
 The dead planetary hour.

Two crystal planes, three inches square,
 Steeped in the blood of milk-white fowl,
With careful skill he did prepare,
 'Gainst next should hoot the midnight owl.

One would reveal the summoned Fay,
 Who, by her-divining art
Should on the second plane display
 Scenes to grieve, or cheer, his heart.

N 5

Thus endowed to conjure fairie,
  He would fain have conjured sleep,
But the god of lovers, wary,
  Hovers not o'er eyes that weep.

Sad and restless all the morning,
  Sad and restless all the noon,
Counting every chime of warning
  Through the longest day of June:

Thus he lingered, thus he wandered,
  Round about his lady's hall,
Till his hopes were nearly foundered—
  Till a rival spoke his fall.

In an oriel he saw her,
  Chatting, smiling, blooming gay ;
Doating, maddening, he bewailed her,
  Doubting his first doubts this day.

Breathing lilacs after showers,
  Bending with the silver drops,

Greenest leaves and purple flowers,
  Waving where the goldfinch hops,

And scattering round the scented dew,
  And sparkling on the sunny air,
Not half so fresh as Aura glow,
  Not half so graceful—half so fair.

Too soon she vanished from his eyes,
  And Evening summoned him afar,
Then to the high-browed Park he hies;
  There, must he meet the twilight-star.

With magic mirrors, hazel wand,
  Eyelids touched with clearing spell,
He sought the Court of Fairie land,
  Hidden in their distant dell.

Through the shaded walks so wide,
  That climb about the southern hill,
Edwy passed with rapid stride.
  Nor saw one Elf—though all was still.

With toil he gained the airy brow,
　　And, panting, paused to breathe awhile,
And throw a lingering look below
　　O'er the still landscape's parting smile.

Crowning the long vista's shade,
　　O'ertopped with turrets, terraced high,
Windsor all its pomp displayed,
　　Beneath the glowing western sky.

Beyond, the low, blue hills repose,
　　Along the far horizon's bound.
How soft the hues the forest throws,
　　Its leafy darkness shedding round !

Those hills their stretching woods display
　　In faint shade, through the azure veil,
While, sweetly bright, the setting ray
　　Bids many a spire once more—farewell.

And farewell to the banner proud,
　　That o'er the broad Keep floats on air,

Proclaiming, as with trumpet loud,
  It's royal lord reposes there.

Pale and more pale the scene retires,
  And Windsor's state has vanished now,
Save one dim tower, that boldly spires
  To meet the star on twilight's brow.

There stood he tranced, till, in the air,
  Warbled music passed along;
So softly sweet, so finely clear!
  This was sure a Fairie song.

For, now no woodlark waked to sing;
  Every little eye was closed;
On slender foot, with drooping wing,
  In it's home each bird reposed.

Save one, and, where he winged his way,
  Pleased, Edwy heard his strain advance,
On his smooth neck a Fairie lay,
  Or rather did a Fairie dance.

A veil of gossamer she wore,
    All spangled round with primrose dew ;
A star-beam for a wand she bore,
    Which she from Venus slyly drew.

This little bird on circling pinions
    Wantoned over Edwy's head,
Then to its shady, loved dominions,
    With its Fairie lady sped.

The while his Fairie lady trills
    " To the beech-woods follow me,
Up the lawns and o'er the hills,
    To the high woods follow me."

In tiny echoes " Follow me"
    All the hills and glades prolong ;
From every bush and hollow tree
    Seemed to rise the choral song.

And Edwy, round each hollow tree,
    Spied the motley Elves at play ;

While, thick as emmets, " Follow me,"
   They sang again, and passed away.

O'er greenest lawns, through proudest groves,
   He pursued his feathered guide,
O'er scenes, that silent Moonlight loves,
   To the long lake's* mossy side.

The little bird flew o'er the lake ;
   Edwy round the turf-banks went,
Close where the silver currents break,
   And lower oaks their branches bent.

The stream is there with rocks inlaid ;
   He tripped o'er these, and reached the road,
That, broad and turfy 'neath the shade,
   Leads to the pleasantest abode.

* The Virginia Water in Windsor Great Park. The Author was so frequently in the scenes alluded to, between the years 1810 and 1814, that the ideas, which this and the preceding and succeeding pieces show, may be safely dated from that period.—Ed.

Green above green, of every hue,
   The bordering trees in vista bend,*
Shrubs lay their low leaves on the dew,
   And pine and larch on light ascend.

Galleries of verdure ! all is green,
   Here lawn and bending boughs below ;
Above 'tis stately shade ; the scene
   Seems made for glancing, Fairie show.

But, closer bowered, their noonday haunt
   Rests in a hollow, beechen dell ;
It's marge no human hand could plant,
   It's shadows seem to breathe a spell.

Now, would you view the Fairies' scene,
   Where twilight-dances print the lawn,
Where it spreads out in softest green,
   To gaps, whence distant landscapes dawn.

* The beautiful lodge at Sandpit Gate opening from the
Western side of the Great Park. The scenery about this is
of exceeding beauty and sweet repose.

Hie to the western forest-gate ;
　There Claudian beauty melts around ;
There Elfin-turrets keep their state,
　And tell, at once, 'tis Fairie ground.

Or, at that later Evening-hour ;
　When the turf gladdens with the dew,
That almost darkens Windsor's tower,
　And gives near hills a distant blue.

And oh ! if Silence could be seen,
　Thus would she look, so meek, so pale,
The image of this very scene,
　When Evening glances on the vale.

Now Edwy reached the wood-walks wild,*
　That open from the watery glade,

---

* The beautiful turf-walks, that branch from the Virginia
Water, exhibit, perhaps, every known variety of pine and fir
on their long, sweeping borders. Their stately forms and the
variety of their tints, intermixed, at intervals, with lofty oak
and beech, and so closely bowered below with flowering shrubs,
that scarcely a spot of earth is visible beneath them, make
these broad, green alleys as delightful, when closely viewed,
as they are otherwise graceful from their general aspect.

Where sweet vale-lilies, violets mild,
　And primrose tufts the grass inlaid.

Climbing the spiky blades and stems,
　Gathering dews, were Elves a million,
Diamond drops and crystal gems,
　To fringe their Fairie Queen's pavilion.

And see what flaming lights appear !
　Flashed through the foliage arching high ;
What silver horn winds, sweet and clear,
　As breathing from the lips of Joy !

Sudden the elves, on flower and blade,
　Forsake their task, and, with a bound,
Touch the green turf, and down the glade
　Take hands and trip a welcome round.

But Edwy hears no more the strain
　Of his fleeting, tiny lady,
And watches for her bird, in vain,
　To lead him through the alleys shady.

By him an elfin-courier speeds
  On grasshopper his forest-ways ; .
Brushing the humble cowslip heads,
  While each its trembling homage pays.

And next, a winged beetle came,
  Sounding deep his herald-horn,
The fairy sovereign to proclaim,
  And evil sprites away to warn.

There, whisked an Indian lanthorn-fly
  Quick flashing forth it's emerald sheen ;
Dancing low and dancing high,
  In many a ring of fiery green.

Then came a creeping, stilly breeze,
  That made the crisped waters live,
That shivered all the sleeping trees,
  And bade the leaves their essence give.

But see, the birds on every bough
  Awake and stretch their ruffled wings ;

And o'er the dewy turf below
  His starry glance the glow-worm flings;

And the whole woodbank's flowery couch
  Is sprinkled now with glimmering bands,
Waiting their tiny Queen's approach,
  Her guards and lights to Fairie lands.

Again, that horn of Joy breathes fine,
  Again, the moonlight-light waters shake;
Where'er the foaming tips combine,
  Rises a fairy of the lake.

Half veiled within the sparkling strife,
  His inexperienced eyes scarce see
The pale forms changing into life,
  Till all is glowing pageantry.

True to their sovereign's summons they,
  Upon the lake's enchanted shore,
Await her presence proud and gay,
  Where rides the fleet to waft her o'er.

And now a spicy, rare perfume,
  Such as breathes from Indian dells,
Fills all the high-wood's leafy dome,
  And the fine Fairie presence tells.

And faint aërial strains are heard,
  As through the rich, festooning ways,
The Queen in moonlit-pomp appeared,
  Amongst ten thousand dancing Fays.

By gold and purple butterflies
  Her rose-leaved car was drawn in air;
Above, two birds of Paradise
  Arch o'er her head their plumage rare.

While, far around her, dancing beams,
  That with bright rainbow colours glow,
Strike on the gloom in transient gleams,
  And all her elfin-escort show.

All in the busy air around
  Pert eyes and little wings are seen,

And voices whisper, feathers sound,
   Attendant on their elfin-queen.

A robe of silvery snow she wore,
   Frosted with magic art so true,
That the hot breath of Midsummer
   Could never change it into dew.

And, wafted by her happy bird,
   A courtier-fairy oft proclaims,
" Now let the mirthful song be heard ;
   Our lady queen a welcome claims."

The little bird too 'gan to sing,
   And then the fairy tried her voice ;
As gaily as the airs of Spring
   Did that poor little bird rejoice.

The measure changed, a languid call,
   Sweet with sorrow, thrice it sounded,
Concluding in a dying fall,
   Softer than e'er fountain rounded.

" O Nightingale ! it was thy song
   Sent through the woods that dying close ;
I know thee now ; the note prolong ;
   Oh ! speak again those tender woes !"

Under the boughs, the elfin-train
   Mutely listened to the measure ;
But, when he trilled his joy again,
   They beat the ground in antic pleasure.

" O bird of feeling, various, sweet !
   Thee and thy guardian-friend I hail ;
I KNOW THEE NOW, and gladly greet
   The Love-Fay and her nightingale.

All fly before the elfin-queen,
   Toward the lake's high-crowned head,
Near where the forest-oaks begin
   A reverential gloom to spread.

With thousand sparks the woodbank swarms :
   Her glow-worm knights, in long array,

Marshalled by Fire-fly—King at Arms,
  Guard her and light her on her way.

Where'er they move, the drowsy flowers
  Unclose their leafy curtains far;
And Fays, asleep within their bowers,
  Leap forth, and dance before her car;

Dance to that crystal lake's green side,
  That winds through fir-crowned lawns and woods,
Whose beeches old, in giant pride,
  Fling their broad shadows on the floods.

And oft they wantoned with the surge,
  That, flowing near the Fairie court,
It's silver line on line did urge,
  As if to tempt and share their sport;

As if to woo the elfin-queen,
  To float upon its moonlight breast;
Pleased to unfold each margent scene,
  And bear her to her bower of rest.

The smile, that played upon it's face,
　She seemed by magic lore to read;
And, with a kind and sportive grace,
　She bade her tiny sailors speed.

A fleet of pleasure-boats lay there,
　Such vessels as befit a sprite;
The water-lilies schooners were,
　Leaf after leaf out-spreading white.

There skiffs, fresh gathered from the lime:
　There acorn-barges broad and deep;
So safe, that, e'en in tempest-time,
　An Elf upon his oars might sleep,

And in his HEART of OAK could go,
　His tiny DREADNOUGHT, singing gay,
Spite of the winds and rocks below,
　Round every fairy cliff and bay.

Sweet wherries of long lavender,
　Blossoms of every shape and stain,

From blue-bell yachts to bird-pepper,
  Attended for the courtier-train.

But their bright Queen more proudly sailed
  In a pearl-shell ship of the line :
By water mouse-ear was she veiled,
  And she was fanned with eglantine.

Her canopy, bedropped with gold,
  Had floated on the Indian tide ;
A lotos-leaf, with ample fold,
  Swelled for her sail, in snowy pride.

The cordage was of silver thread
  Spun of fine bark of ashen tree ;
The mast of sandal wood ; the head
  A living dolphin seemed to be.

Her green knights watched upon the shrouds,
  Or ranged them far along the prow ;
Stood round their Queen, in radiant crowds,
  Or gleamed far on the wave below.

And others, ranked as on a cone,
　Stage above stage, of towery height,
Moved on the lake around her throne,
　Proud, floating pyramids of light.

Above them all, then might you spy,
　In busy care, high o'er the mast,
Their king-at-arms, Sir Lanthorn-fly,
　Ordering the pageant, as it past;

And, glancing down the moonlight air,
　He checked the lily-schooner's way;
And, whisking here and whisking there,
　Recalled each blossom-sail astray.

Then, self-triumphant, in the van,
　In airy circles pleased he danced;
Yet, while he led the revel on,
　Back, for his Queen's applauses glanced.

And thus in gliding state she went
　O'er the long windings of the wave,

Where many a watchful eye was bent,
  From hollow oak and secret cave.

The screech-owl and the snake were there,
  The boding raven, cruel kite,
That fill the timid heart with care,
  And love to prowl in moonless night.

But chief on the old Forest's bound,
  Where the still waters sink away,
Such evil agents walk their round,
  Or lurk within the oaks so grey.

Bewildered in the wild-wood glades,
  Edwy oft lost the long lake's side;
Till, through some deep grove's opening shades,
  He saw the splendid vision glide.

Low glanced the silver oars along,
  Quick came the spires of glow-worm light,
That round their Queen's tall galley throng,
  Shooting long beams aslant the night;

These, trembling through the branches' dome,
　　Touching each leaf with transient joy,
Now seen, now lost, from gloom to gloom,
　　Showed like the stars, when clouds fleet by.

Then, over banks and under woods,
　　Edwy pursued the pageant's way;
Till, having reached the smiling floods,
　　The frolick shores his hopes betray.

For, winding back, his course they mar,
　　Leaving him on some jutting steep,
'Mid the lone waters, while afar
　　The inmost bay the Fairies sweep.

And thus through wilds and woods he toiled,
　　Lured by short glimpse of that bright train,
Which through the distant shadows smiled,
　　As if in mockery of his pain.

Till, once again, he heard remote
　　That gentle bird, faithful to lovers;

And, following the high-warbled note,
  Again the Fairie fleet discovers:

Just as it touched the farther shore,
  To land the Queen those groves among;
When still was every little oar,
  And every white sail breathless hung.

No sound was heard but Music's voice,
  Roused by the motley elfin-band,
Who play in moonshine, and rejoice
  In choral welcomes o'er the strand.

The groves, that hovered o'er the brink,
  The polished lake more dark returns;
And each bright star, in emerald twink,
  Beneath the wave more keenly burns.

And there, the rival of their beams,
  Reflected by the glass below,
A shooting-star Sir Fire-fly seems,
  While marshalling the Fairie show.

Each shroud and sail of Fairie bark,
   Each glittering oar and image fair,
Within that mirror, blue and dark,
   Lay, like a picture, pencilled fair.

But when Sir Fire-fly's knights moved on,
   And their green torches mutely raised,
Then all the Fairie's splendour shone,
   And shores and woods and waters blazed.

Thus, ranged in vista-lines of light,
   Moving beneath the leafy gloom,
Where forest-oaks spread deepest night,
   They guard her to her sylvan home.

Under an ancient beech, that high
   Out-hung it's spray, her dreams of night
Were veiled from every curious eye,
   Save when with magic virtue bright.

It's mighty boughs a circle filled;
   Like necromantic guard it stood;

It's air severe the wanderer chilled,
  It's frown and haughty attitude.

Soon as that beechen shade she reached,
  Rustled its every leaf for joy ;
Then gracefully her wand she stretched,
  And lighted all its leaves on high.

Yet flame of torch, or lamp, was none,
  Nor any glittering sparkle there ;
It seemed as if the setting sun
  Tinged the rich spray with rosy air.

Her bower through many chambers ranged,
  And each a different purpose showed ;
This, oft with mystic shadows changed ;
  That, for the dance, or banquet, glowed.

Beyond them all, her cell of rest
  In verdant shade and silence lay ;
Save, when the ring-dove in her nest
  Sung all her gentle cares away :

And sleepy leaves, scarce moved in air,
　Or only swayed by breezes fleet,
With the lake's murmuring falls afar,
　Made melody most sad and sweet.

Lime-blossoms strewed the mossy floor,
　And breathed a dewy fragrance round,
Inviting her to slumbers pure,
　While freshness seemed to bless the ground.

Yet here, sometimes, this Queen of dreams
　Would weave such seeming forms of fate,
As, sent upon the still moonbeams,
　Oft by the midnight sleeper wait.

Hid in her cool bower might she view
　The noontide lake and sunny lawns;
The slow sail on the waters blue,
　And, through the brakes, the fleeting fawns;

And watch them on the watery brim,
　Bending to sip the dainty wave,

o 5

Then starting at the form so slim,
  The shadowed crystal truly gave.

Unseen, she traced each step that roved
  Rejoicing on that margent green ;
Or sought the hills and groves beloved,
  That crown with pleasant shade the scene.

Edwy had joined the Fairie's train,
  Just as she reached her leafy dome,
While full arose the choral strain
  Of welcome to her beechen home.

Her glow-worm knights, wide round the beech,
  In glimmering circles take their stand ;
Adder, nor bird of boding speech,
  Nor step unblest may pass that band.

In front, high on the beechen spray,
  Like Hesper, on the eastern dawn,
Sir Fire-fly spreads his watchful ray
  O'er dell obscure and distant lawn.

No shape, among the shadows there,
  Could glide unseen, nor move, where frowned
That beech's wizard brows in air,
  And shrink not from the mystic ground.

Save Edwy, with his magic spell;—
  Invisible and fearless, he
Might pass e'en to the Fairie's cell,
  Unknown—but of one enemy.

She tripped into her vestibule,
  Arched high with rose and eglantine,
Breathing a fragrance light and cool,
  And bright with dew-drops, crystalline.

Here many a bell, that, in the day,
  Had hung its fainting head awry,
Now waked for her in beauty gay,
  And breathed for her its perfumed sigh.

Her pavilion next she entered ;
  Clear the glassy columns shone ;

To the turf steps Edwy ventured,
  And beheld her on her throne.

Under an ebon arch reclining,
  With brilliant drops all thickly hung,
Where Mimosa's leaves were twining,
  She listened, while the Love-Fay sung.

The thousand dew-drops hanging there
  And in the swelling dome, on high,
Trembled with radiance keen and fair,
  Poured from her living diamond's eye.

Splendour and Joy around her moved,
  And winning smiles beamed in her face,
And every virtue most beloved
  Gave to her air a tender grace.

On the ruby-pavement stealing,
  Circling Elves their homage gave,
Then, in quaint moriscoes reeling,
  They dance, and airy garlands wave.

The silver-triangle, the lute,
  The tambourine, with tiny bells,
Mix with the softly-breathing flute;
  The mellow horn more distant swells.

A quaint and various group arrived:
  One, fliting on a bat's wing came,
No orchard, where he haunted, thrived;
  Malignant Elfant was his name.

One, upon a field-mouse gliding,
  Oft the traveller appalled,
Wondrously his steps misguiding;
  Sly Elféna she was called.

A third, upon a squirrel springing,
  Never rested, night, or day;
Into some droll mischief bringing
  Solemn heads, as well as gay.

On butterfly next sailed a Fairie;
  She soothes fine ladies in their vapour,

Who of unchanging good are weary,
　And weep, because they've nought to weep for.

Winged by an owl, there came an elf,
　Who loved to haunt the study-table,
Where, full of grave, important self,
　The wisest head he would disable.

And make it Pro-and-Con and fight
　On subjects lofty as the steeple ;
Or tempt some Witling to endite
　Long dreams, about the elfin-people !

And now, the Fairie Queen demanded
　Whether her elves the tasks had done,
That, at sun-set, she had commanded ;
　And now she called them one by one.

She called them, but they came not all ;
　Again, the magic horn was wound,
Then thronging sprites obeyed the call ;
　But still some truants wild were found.

Yet was this blast so distant heard,
  That elves, on Windsor's battlement,
Mounted the moonbeams at it's word,
  And o'er the Long Walk gaily went ;

Nor stayed upon the tufts to dance
  Of the broad, bowery way, that swept,
With utmost pomp, beneath their glance,
  Though there the yellow moonlight slept ;

Though many a bird they loved was hid
  In silent rest, beneath the leaves,
Which, if awaked and gently bid,
  Would sing the song that care deceives—

Yet, had they surely waked them, too,
  And danced a morrice on the trees,
Had not the horn complaining blew,
  Like coming of a tempest breeze.

But e'en the Fairie's summons failed,
  Yielding awhile to Beauty's spell,

When Windsor's proudest groves they hailed,
  Crowning its wildest, deepest dell.

They paused a moment on that brow,
  Under the shading oaks they strayed,
To spy, beneath the branches low,
  The moonlight-towers, beyond their shade.

Beyond that shade in peace they lay,
  Gates, turrets, battlements aloft,
Just silvered by the distant ray,
  That 'neath the dark boughs glimmered oft.

It seemed some vision of the air,
  By magic raised in forest lone,
That held entranced some lady fair,
  Till nodding towers her knight should own.

The horn again ! but not like breeze
  Before some gentle summer shower,
But rushing through th' affrighted trees,
  E'en with an angry whirlwind's power.

The moonlight-castle sinks and fades,
 Beneath the tossing boughs afar ;
And fear the truant elves invades ;
 And swift they mount their beamy car.

No banquet in the bower for them ;
 No tripping strains their steps invite ;
The Fairie sovereign will condemn
 Their disobedience and their slight.

" Hence," she cries, " a vision weave
 For the couch of that false lover,
Who could a trusting heart deceive ;
 Hence, and o'er his slumber hover.

" Dance before him, like a shade ;
 Trace upon his sleeping eye
Image of that mournful maid,
 Whom he won, and left to die ;

" In my cell of shadows look
 You will there the semblance see,

Of the damsel he forsook
  All from idle vanity.

" Touch his heart with jealousy,
  Shape a dream to rouse despair ;
Then to the sad maiden flee,
  And expel her silly care.

" So, when the streaky dawn doth wake,
  Each shall rise, with changed intent ;
Each shall the other's fortune take,
  He, despair—and she, content.

" If these dreams ye shadow well,
  Return, before the lark is up,
Or the chime of matin bell ;
  Dance the morrice ; sip the cup.

                        " Now farewell."

Scarce had she spoke, when all the bower
  As in a twilight shadow lay ;
The dewy lamp on every flower
  Quivered first, then died away.

Her magic diamond warned the Queen
   Of step unhallowed passing near ;
It paled its ray to trembling green,
   And shrunk with sympathetic fear.

Then hastily the Queen exclaimed,
   " Some mortal footsteps press the ground ;"
For Edwy, when the Elves she named,
   Had nearer drawn to catch the sound.

Just then the little Nightingale,
   In pity of the lover's pain,
Sung from Mimosa's shadowy veil
   His softest, sweetest, saddest tale.

Which, well he knew, his Queen would win
   From aught ungracious, or severe.
With charmed, attentive, brow serene,
   She smiled, and, dashing off a tear,

On Eda called, the Love Fay, thrice,
   Some tale of mortal truth to tell :—

Her name did Edwy's heart rejoice;
　　For, that Fay's name completes his spell!

Then straight, the bower began to show
　　Returning light; and, through each bud,
From faintness freed to living glow,
　　Circled the bright transparent blood.

Now what of chastisement befell
　　This vagrant swain, for his intrusion,
Village-tradition does not tell,
　　Or tells with most profound confusion.

But this most gossips do relate,
　　That, though he was not held in durance,
He gained no knowledge of his fate,
　　And nothing got by his assurance,

Unless it be, that he did see
　　What seldom had been seen before,
A Fairie Court, in starlight sport,
　　With pleasure squadrons and on shore.

But haply, on some other day,
  We may learn more of his manœuvres,
And then we shall not fail to say,
  What came of Aura and her lovers.

PART III.

THE MAGIC MIRRORS.

A SUMMER NIGHT IN WINDSOR FOREST.

Edwy forsook the Fairie Court,
   And to forest-glades withdrew,
Where never yet had elfin-sport
   Cheered the melancholy view.

Upon the hazel-wands he writes
   Eda's name, with " thrice and three,"
Then buries them, with bidden rites,
   Underneath a forest-tree.

It was an oak, whose trunk within
   A foul and watching spirit lay,

Whose night-shrieks in the tempest-din,
  Filled the traveller with dismay:

It was an oak, whose sinewy boughs
  Threw a dark horror o'er the ground;
Whose high, gaunt top and warrior-brows
  With the storms of ages frowned.

Its trunk was never touched with light,
  So wide and deep the branching shade
Of leaves, that, on a starry night,
  A gleam, like break of morning, shed.

But the brook, stealing from the brake,
  Showed a glimpse of brighter ray,
When on it's dewy banks did take
  Will-o'-the Wisp his mystic way.

Round the high roots our Edwy drew,
  With muttered charm, a magic line;
And in the circle heart's ease threw,
  And briony and eglantine;

Then sweets and poisons, three and three,
  Jess'mine blossoms, violet bud,
The deadly nightshade's tresses grey,
  And the pale Monk's gloomy head.

Next, the buried wands he raised,
  And " Eda! Eda! Eda!" called;
Thrice upon the West he gazed,
  When, hark! a shriek his breast appalled.

It was the spirit of the oak,
  Who, startled by the Love-Fay's name,
His dark and secret home forsook.
  He fled, in haste, whene'er she came.

A tongue from Windsor's distant tower
  Tolled Twelve along the silent wood,
When, lo! the planet of the hour
  Quivered upon the trembling flood.

Cheered by the monitory sight,
  Then Edwy forth his mirrors drew,

And by that star's informing light,
  Upheld them to his searching view.

Again he called on Eda's name
  Mildly and meekly to appear.
And round the crystals rolled a flame;
  While unknown murmurs met his ear.

See !—o'er the mirrors mists arise,
  And strange and fearful shadows throng;
Frowning faces, glaring eyes
  Look and threat and glance along.

These gone, a tiny form there bounds,
  Flitting along the magic glass;
Which, in an instant, her surrounds
  With leaves of Love in Idleness.

She seems reclining in a bower,
  As the green leaves around her spread,
The motley-yellow, purple flower
  Bends in a top-knot o'er her head.

As round this cage of wreaths she hies,
  Forth from her wand a lustre pale
Dawns o'er her blue and frolic eyes,
  And silvers all her dewy veil,

Touches the rose upon her cheek,
  The dimple, that her quaint lip owns,
The smile, that now begins to break,
  Through clouds of wild, capricious frowns.

While Edwy gazed, a little strain
  Of sweet complaint did feebly swell,
When, hovering round her leafy chain,
  Behold! her faithful Nightingale!

He perched upon the true-knot there,
  And tried to break, with slender bill,
Her prison-wreath, so flowery fair;
  But the leaves mocked his puny skill.

Too late, she owns the forceful spell
  The little purple blossom throws.

Fixed, as a painting, she must tell
  Mildly and meekly all she knows !

" Fairy Eda ! show to me
  Aura, as she 's now employed."—
" On the other glass you 'll see ;"
  With pretty lisp the Fay replied.

He looked ; the colours faintly dawn,
  And living forms begin to glow :
Aura, full-dressed in lace and lawn,
  Blooms in a ball-room with a beau.

And, dancing with a Grace's air,
  And with the eyes of Venus smiling,
Edwy beheld her, with despair,
  His hated rival's heart beguiling.

To atoms he had almost dashed
  The mirror, and so lost the spell,
But warning lights around him flashed,
  Checked his hand, and all was well,

" Who is this Fop, so light and vain ?" —
　　Quickly, the magic scene is changed
To rivers, woods, a wide domain,
　　With falconers on the banks ranged.

All at their head his rival pranced
　　In velvet cap, with feathers gay,
And proudly o'er the sward advanced,
　　While men and steeds their lord.obey.

" O tell me, Eda—loves she him ?
　　Can she her promise old forget ?"—
A flame curled round the mirror's rim ;
　　The crystal darkened into jet.

And in long moonlight prospect rose
　　Windsor.Terrace, flanked with towers ;
How soft the lights and shades repose
　　Among the low Park's lawns and bowers !

Oh ! what an arch the heavens throw
　　Upon the vast horizon round !

The stars ! how numberless they glow
 Down to the landscape's dim-seen bound !

Some battlements are left in night ;
 Others almost appear to shine
Of yonder tower, whose stately height
 Draws on the sky a tall black line,

That measures, on the azure void,
 Billions of miles, while worlds unknown,
Distant howe'er, glow, side by side,
 Upon it's shadowy profile shown.

Down on the terrace, men appear,
 Gliding along the stately wall,
With arms enfolding the tall spear—
 How still their measured footsteps fall !

Voices are heard round that vast shade,
 Although no talkers meet the sight ;
But, beyond, where moonbeams spread,
 Figures steal upon the light.

'Twas Aura, with a lady-friend—
   'Twas Aura, with this lover new!
Ah! does she to his suit attend?
   The distance baffled Edwy's view.

" Eda! Eda! why torment me
   With obscure ambiguous truth?
Thou to show my fate wast sent me.
   Say, will she wed this fopling-youth?"

Behold! the terrace fades away!
   And a tap'stried room succeeds;
Her sire, with age and wisdom grey,
   'Mid lawyer, settlements and deed

Again, the charmed picture changed:
   A gothic porch, with silk all hung;
There beaux and ladies fair are ranged,
   While humbler gazers round them throng.

There a happy rival waited
   With his friends, in trim array:

" Aura ! what makes thee belated ?
    Aura ! why this long delay ?"

Again, the mirrors were in danger,
    From our thoughtless Edwy's rage ;
But a fairie checked his anger—
    Would she might his grief assuage !

Next, dimly on the crystal steals
    A chamber in her father's home ;
There, Aura, weeping, pleads and kneels !
    The father, frowning, quits the room.

Again the changeful glass receives
    The porch—and Edwy, doth he tremble,
As smiling Aura there he sees ?
    And whom doth the bridegroom resemble ?

It is—*himself !*—He 's joyous, frantic,
    As the glass showed his happy shape ;
But as he sprung, with gesture antic,
    It fell, and let the fairie 'scape !

Without due homage let her fly !
 Straight, unknown voices from the ground
Wildly exclaimed, " O fie ! fie ! fie !"
 And " Fie ! fie ! fie !" the echoes sound.

Unhomaged he had let her fly !
 From the old oak an owlet hooted ;
And thence a louder "Fie ! fie ! fie !"
 To the spot poor Edwy rooted.

But, soon recovered, through the woods,
 Hopeful and light, away he sprung :
The moon peeped through their leafy hoods,
 And o'er the path her chequers flung.

To the forest's-edge he hied,
 Where the Beech's giant-form
Had, for age on age, defied,
 With his lion-fangs the storm :

Where the Lime, with spotted bark—
 Spots, that old moss on silver weaves,

Hung her spray on branches dark
　　Among the light transparent leaves,

And fragrant blossoms, forming bowers,
　　That cast, at noon, a twilight green,
Where 'twas most sweet to watch the hours
　　Change the highly-tinctured scene.

The silvery Aspin quivered nigh,
　　The spiry Pine in darkness rose,
The Ash, all airy grace, on high
　　Waved her lightly-feathered boughs.

And there the mighty Chesnut reared
　　His massy verdure, deepening night;
Whose pale flowers through the dark appeared
　　Like gleams of April's coldest light.

Under the low boughs Edwy went.
　　Shade, after shade, in close array,
A sadder tint to midnight lent;
　　And thoughtless Edwy lost his way.

Now, far beyond the long-drawn gloom,
  Where a faint, misty moonlight fell,
He watched a lonely figure roam,
  And loud he made the echoes swell.

His call was heard, the stranger turned,
  And paused a moment; but, in vain,
Our Edwy would his way have learned,
  For, not a word in answer came.

The vision fled—but soon a cry,
  Loud, though far-off, alarmed his ear;
And a footstep passed him by;
  Which he followed fast and near.

Till a groan of sad affright
  Almost killed him, with dismay;
And to his undoubting sight
  There a man expiring lay.

As, horror-fixed, awhile he stood,
  A cloud o'erspread it's darkening veil;

It suited well his fearful mood ;
   It hid that dreadful visage pale.

Now, mark, where yonder high elms crowd,
   What red lights gleam and pass along !
What funeral torches, dirges loud !
   A bier and mourners round it throng.

Down th' avenue of pines they go :
   All sad and chaunting their despair,
Then wind they on in pomp of woe ;
   Then fade and vanish into air !

For, yonder, o'er the eastern hill,
   Morning's crystal tint is seen,
Edging the darkness, solemn still,
   And glimmering o'er the sleeping scene.

O best of light ! O light of soul !
   O blessed Dawn, to thee we owe
The humbled thought—our mind's best dole,
   The bliss of praise—Devotion's glow.

O blessed Dawn ! more sweet to me
  Thy gradual hues, thy influence fine
O'er flying darkness, than the ray
  And glorious pomp, that doth enshrine

The cope of heaven, when the Sun
  Comes laughing from the joyous East,
And bids th' expressive shadows run
  To tell his coming to the West.

At thy first tint the happy lark
  Awakes, and trills his note of joy ;
And feebler, warbling murmurs, hark !
  Break from the woodlands—rise, and die,

At thy first tint, O blessed light !
  Th' observant Elves and spectres fled,
And that misguiding, watching sprite
  Home to her oaken dungeon sped ;

Elfena then, the mischief-fay,
  Who with an urchin had combined

To 'wilder Edwy thus astray;
   Now in a Monk's-hood is confined.

No dying man was there—no moan,
   There were no red-lights, near the elms,
No funeral torches, dirge's moan,
   No sable band, whom grief o'erwhelms.

Still, doubtful of his homeward way,
   Our hero watched the rise of dawn,
Over a beech-tree's airy spray,
   That trembles on the Park's high lawn.

And soon the glorious Sun was spied,
   And Windsor, in her pomp of groves,
Rose up in battlemented pride,
   Queen of the vale, that Old Thames loves—

From where the far-seen western hill
   In smiling slumber seems to lie,
Upon the azure vault so still
   As listening heaven's harmony,

To where, beneath the eastern ray,
  With swelling dome and spires aloft,
Vast London's lengthened city lay,
  All miniatured, distinct and soft—

To where, upon the northern edge,
  Learned Harrow points her vane,
And Stanmore lifts it's heathy ridge,
  Sloping to the cultured plain,

Which, purpled with the morning's glow,
  To boundless tints of azure fades,
While humbler spires and hamlets show
  Their sun-lights o'er the woody shades ;

And gleaming Thames along the vale,
  'Midst willowy meads, his waters led,
While, here and there, a feeble sail
  Was to the scarce-felt breeze outspread.

The willowy meads and lawns rejoice ;
  And every heath, and warbling wood ;

The fragrant air, with whispering voice,
　The golden clouds, the brightened flood,

All laugh and sing beneath the morn,
　The dancing lamb, the springing deer ;
The wild bee with his humming horn,
　And, loud and long, Sir Chanticleer.

Soon as his joyous clarion calls,
　Answering notes strike up and swell
From rafter dark and loop-holed walls,
　Where sleep and silence seemed to dwell,

Surprising with their clamour clear
　The passing herdsman and his hound ;
Thus, far and near, Sir Chanticleer
　Rouses up all the country round.

Edwy so roused, who long had stood
　Over this scene of morning beauty,
Forgetting every other good,
　And lost to each forgotten duty,

Now, bounding lightly down the hills
  And through the high o'erarching groves,
Hied to his home, where Eda wills
  He soon shall wed the nymph he loves;

And grateful for the boon she grants,
  He now resolves, that, never more,
His spell shall shock her quiet haunts;
  And quite abjures the magic lore.

But,—never let impatient wight,
  When he presumes to woo a fairie,
Destroy his glass,—or rouse her spite,
  But civil be—and very wary.

        Thus all was well,
        As watchmen tell,
  Of fairie sports in Windsor glades,
        Save that too long
        A summer-song
  Once lingered in those witching shades.

SCENE ON THE NORTHERN SHORE
OF SICILY.

HERE, from the Castle's terraced site,
  I view, once more, the varied scene
  Of hamlets, woods, and pastures green,
And vales far stretching from the sight.
Beneath the tints of coming night;
  And there is misty ocean seen,
  With glancing oars and waves serene,
And stealing sail of shifting light.
Now, let me hear the shepherd's lay,
  As on some bank he sits alone ;
  That oaten reed, of tender tone,
He loves, at setting sun, to play.
It speaks in Joy's delightful glee ;
  Then Pity's strains its breath obey—
Or Love's soft voice it seems to be—
  And steals at last the soul away !

And now, the village bells afar
  Their melancholy music sound
Mournfully o'er the waters round,
  Till Twilight sends her trembling star.
Oft shall my pensive heart attend,
  As swell the notes along the breeze,
And weep anew the buried friend,
  In tears, that sadly, softly please;
And, when pale moonlight tips the trees,
  On the dark Castle's tower ascends,
Throws o'er it's walls a silvery gleam,
  And in one soft confusion blends
Forest and mountain, plain and stream,
  I list the drowsy sounds, that creep
On night's still air, to soothe the soul;
  The hollow moan of Ocean's roll,
The bleat and bell of wandering sheep,
  The distant watch-dog's feeble bark,
The voice of herdsman pacing home
  Along the leafy labyrinth dark,
And sounds, that from the Castle come
  Of closing door, that sullen falls,

And murmurs, through the chambers high
  Of half-sung strains from ancient halls,
That through the long, long galleries die.
And now the taper's flame I spy
  In antique casement, glimmering pale;
And now 'tis vanished from my eye,
  And all but gloom and silence fail.

Once more, I stand in pensive mood,
  And gaze on forms, that Truth delude;
And still, 'mid Fancy's flitting scene,
  I catch the streaming cottage-light,
Twinkling the restless leaves-between,
  And Ocean's flood, in moonbeams bright.

FINIS.

LONDON:
PRINTED BY S. AND R. BENTLEY, DORSET-STREET.

LaVergne, TN USA
08 October 2010
200125LV00003B/49/A